THE FREEDOM PROJECT

OTHER BOOKS BY WILKO VAN DE KAMP

The Freedom Project
Travel
Happiness
Love

A View to Take Home
On My Way
The Wealthy Artist
Author Success Blueprint

These books are available at your local bookstore,
or may be ordered by visiting www.dynamicwindmill.com

Praise for The Freedom Project

Fabulous! You inspire others to embark on the most magnificent journey of their lifetime. Thank you for your insightful contribution.
> Dr. John Demartini, international bestselling author of The Values Factor

Yes! A refreshing book that belongs in the collection of every self respecting human being. Who can't use more love and freedom?
> Dr. Joe Vitale, author of Zero Limits and The Miracle

A must-read for anyone who wants to bring love and freedom in their relationships, at home and at work. If everyone would apply the principles in this book, the world would be a better place!
> Fre3 Fly, Music Producer of the album Fre3dom

I absolutely love this book. It's rare to find such honest advice in such an easily readable and accessible format. This book, which is full of wisdom on what really matters to be truly happy is destined to become a classic.
> Jack Canfield, coauthor of the Chicken Soup for the Soul® series and The Success Principles™

F**k It, I'd buy a copy (if Wilko hadn't sent me a review copy): this brilliant book offers my perfect mix of inspired ideas and strategies with propositions that really made me ponder. Can money really buy 80% of your happiness? Errmmm, how does it work for me? Whatever, I get the feeling that, for the small price of this book, people will be buying a significantly higher % chance of freedom and happiness.

John C. Parkin, author of the F**k It books

Wilko van de Kamp eloquently shares his own journey in "The Freedom Project: Happiness". He will inspire your soul and lift your spirits.

Deborah Sandella PhD, award-winning author
and originator of the RIM Method

Here is a powerhouse book of tips, tactics and approaches for discovering what truly makes you happy, that simply work. A fantastic book which will inspire you to break the mold.

Forrest Willett, author of Baseballs Don't Bounce

This book contains straightforward strategies anyone can use to overcome the key fears associated with stress and unhappiness in a life consumed by work.

Craig Wolfe, president of CelebriDucks

It's about time this book was written. Too many people are stuck in unfulfilling, dead-end careers. This book is the liberating blueprint for finding freedom and happiness in your life.

Charlie Collins, author of Tripping into the Light

The desire to pursue "freedom" could almost be considered universal, regardless of age, race, culture, or gender. But how each of us defines "freedom" is anything but universal. My strong desire to achieve "freedom" in my life helped give me the courage to leave the corporate world to start my own business. However, what I came to realize was how little clarity I actually had on what "freedom" meant to me. What it meant in relation to my business, my relationships, my hobbies, and ultimately my success and happiness. If I could go back in time I would do one thing differently—I would read The Freedom Project. This is a must have book for anyone that wants a step-by-step guide in how to discover and create the "freedom" you truly desire in your life.

Dave Andrews, coauthor of
The 30-Day Sobriety Solution

Wilko and the book he has written is exactly what being an inspirer is all about. It was a pleasure to read and left me feeling, well… inspired.

Mike Stemple, founder of Inspirer

I love Wilko's robust determination and courage to live life on his own terms! I think his book is required reading for anyone who is serious about changing their life, and need's a smart, down-to-earth, owner's manual. Wilko's the best!

                        Carlota Zimmerman, The Creativity Yenta

This book brings out the true meaning of happiness. It is full of tips and tactics and approaches for discovering what truly makes you happy. A fantastic book which will inspire you to break out of you mold and become the person you are truly meant to be. A must read.

                        Jean Ann Reuter, author of Oodles of Love
                        and Success University for Women

THE FREEDOM PROJECT

LOVE 2.0

WILKO VAN DE KAMP

DYNAMIC WINDMILL

The Freedom Project: Love 2.0 by Wilko van de Kamp
Copyright © MMXVIII by Wilko van de Kamp

All rights reserved. No part of this publication may be reproduced, distributed, or transmitted in any form or by any means, including photocopying, recording, or other electronic or mechanical methods, without the prior written permission of the publisher or author, except in the case of brief quotations embodied in critical reviews and certain other noncommercial uses permitted by copyright law. For permission requests, write to the publisher at the address below.

Although every precaution has been taken to verify the accuracy of the information contained herein, the author and/or publisher assume no responsibility for any errors or omissions. No liability is assumed for damages that may result from the use of information contained within.

All reasonable efforts have been made to identify and contact copyright holders but in some cases these could not be traced. If you hold or administer rights for material contained in this book, please contact the publisher. Any errors or omissions will be corrected in subsequent editions.

Quotations are provided by MountainQuotes.com.

Published by:
Dynamic Windmill, PO Box 2751 Stn. M, Calgary, Alberta, T2P 3C2, Canada
www.dynamicwindmill.com

Ordering Information - Quantity sales
Special discounts are available on quantity purchases by corporations, associations, and others. For details, contact the publisher.

ISBN 978-0-9938260-6-1

First Edition

*This book is dedicated to "opa",
my beloved grandfather.*

Contents

Why I wrote this book	15
Living a life by experience	21

Loving The World — 27

My snowboarding adventure	29
An alien perspective to the world	32
Fireworks, resolutions and honesty	38
I'm giving up on being Mr. Persistence	41
The wrong side of the road	43
Celebrating your successes	46
Dream stealers and overcoming fear	48
Feed your curiosity	52
Love and opportunity where you are	55
Let go of some people	57

Loving Your Network — 65

Living the Pura Vida	67
Temptation: there's only one way to find out	72
Latte Art	76
Why I don't believe in job security	80
Entering voluntary solitary confinement	85
Answering the phone	87
Anti-social media: is ignorance truly bliss?	90

Back to school	94

Loving Your Family   *99*

We're all from different countries	101
Creating distance to get closer	103
A detour to Paris and Barcelona	106
Fast-forward eighteen years	110
All you need is love	112
Dealing with death while abroad	115
Weddings and funerals	117
The importance of family	120

Loving Someone Special   *125*

The stage gates of life	127
Lies, damn lies, and statistics	129
Visiting the city of love and light	132
The battle between love and your ego	135
The contradiction of love and freedom	137
The difficulty with marriage	141
Marriage: a death at the altar	144
The Palace of Versailles	148
Is your marriage a good marriage?	152

Loving You   *159*

Escape from the greatest prison in life	161
The art of travel	165
Writing your own life story	169
Rethinking fear	174
Stay true to your personal mission	178

You'll never make it	181
Taking control of your life	185
You already have what it takes	188
Things are different now	193
Parting words	196

Wait... there's more!   199

The Freedom Project Online	200
The zen approach to travel	201
Letting go and moving on	202
My ode to Canada	204
Write A Book	206
About the author	209

Why I wrote this book

An author, who wrote a book about travel hacking, and then another one about happiness at work, now comes forward with a book about love. I'm not denying it's strange. Even more curious is tying the topic of Love to a book series about Freedom. Most people don't associate love with freedom. More and more people choose, or so they say, to be single. They enjoy the freedom it brings them. Why this book?

Let's go a few years back in time. In the fall of 2015 I released my book about Happiness, not expecting that within 24 hours from sharing "Happiness", mine would be taken away. Sometimes what you really want doesn't happen, and what you didn't expect does. Depression and loneliness were on my horizon, together with doubt, fear and a whirlwind of other emotions. Within a week after my book came out there was good news, and bad. The good news: my book had immediately become a number one "hot release" on its first day. The bad? I was back on prescribed anti-depressants. What happened?

One of the first disclaimers I share in my Travel book is that I wouldn't call myself a travel guru. It's the caveat that comes with living a life by experience: don't try this at home. All I attempted to do in that book was to share some of the travel hacking principles that I had consciously and subconsciously developed over many years of exploring our beautiful planet. Nobody tried following my travel advice at home. The book became a number one bestseller and people used my best practice approach to travel. They left their homes, and visited the places they've always wanted to see. Then, in my Happiness book, I shared that I'm not necessarily a big believer in marriage anymore, and even dared announcing that sentence might become a topic for a future book. Be careful what you wish for. You're holding that book right now. And even though by now some have called me a "travel guru", I never expected to be writing about relationships, as I'm definitely not the guy with all the answers when it comes to love.

I made my share of relationship mistakes that I deeply regret. But, as I teach my authors in my book-writing course, most writers don't write because they have the answers, they write because they're looking for answers themselves, which they then share with the world. Just like the first two books in the Freedom Project series, in this third volume I want to do exactly that: share my experiences. Not because they're the ultimate truth, but they've become my truth, and a reality I live by every day. Use them as you see fit.

> *"We are born in one day. We die in one day. We can change in one day. And we can fall in love, in one day. Anything can happen in just one day."*
>
> Gayle Forman

So what happened in the fall of 2015? After traveling and working on my Happiness book all summer, release day was finally there. With the help from many amazing people on my team, I worked hard to make the release a successful one. Our combined efforts paid off, and the book ended its first day as a number one "hot release". I celebrated the success on my patio with a glass of good wine and a cigar, one of my guilty pleasures, while dinner was simmering over the stove. But literally as I was soaking up the rays of sunshine on a warm Calgary afternoon something hit me. I had been completely obsessed with my book. I had once again forgotten about some of the things, and people, that truly mattered to me. I had worked long days, neglecting my girlfriend at that time in the process. Even if you do what you love, it's possible to "over-live" your passion. I had left behind the nine-to-five corporate workforce and pursued a more creative career. On that sunny afternoon after all the hard work was done, I came to the shocking realization that you can still burn yourself out, even if you do what you love most. I promised myself right there and then I'd be better and focus more on the things that truly mattered.

That realization turned out to be too little, too late. Even though my girl believed in my work, and had supported my writing efforts immensely, she decided that day it was enough. While I was preparing dinner, she didn't return home that night, or the next. I was on my own, once again. As I realized what was happening my body went numb. Much like Liz Gilbert in Eat Pray Love I whispered many silent prayers in the days and nights to come. "Oh God I'm in deep trouble here, please help."

What could I do? I had been longing to belong, and that world had been ripped away from underneath me. I wished someone or something would give me a sign on what to do next or where to start walking towards. "Anyone?" I asked. It stayed quiet. I had to let both the future and the past go, and focus on the here and now, today. This book is my story of learning to live by the day and not getting stuck in "what if" scenarios, even though I was very unsure about what the future would hold for me. I tried to live by the day. I told myself, "You are not stuck, you might be just afraid to do what's next". Deep inside me there was a voice that already knew what I really wanted. At the time I just wished it would speak a bit louder.

Life is not easy sometimes, and it will leave you scarred. But I decided this life is my life and I'm going for it. There's so much to celebrate and experience out there that I didn't want to sit down in sadness or depression. Everything you want out of life will lead to an experience. I want to live, and share my experiences with some special people. The question is simple: what do you really want out of life? The goal is to go straight for that. "Love" has to do with finding harmony and bringing it into concert with your life. It's about realizing there's someone who is with you right now who's willing to pick you up. Everything is not always going to be ok. But one thing is true: you do not have to be alone.

With the first two Freedom Project books you'll eventually settle on a standpoint. Travel hacking is easy. Once you get the gist of it, you can apply it over and over again and benefit from free and upgraded travel for the rest of your life. You'll discover yourself how you can expand on the travel principles I teach, and invent new systems. The same goes for happiness at work and creating a meaningful life. For some, it means they start businesses and leave the rat race of nine-to-five corporate offices behind. Others might change their career, or find new ways to give their existing job meaning. After reading my book, people made changes to the way they created a life, and made a living from it. They ended up with a conclusion and found a standpoint that worked for them, or are working towards it.

But with love, it's different. Just like my Happiness book, this book is first of all a collection of observations of the things that did not work for me. I feel like including another "don't try this at home" caveat. But in the end, from what didn't work I extracted a core essence and from there I deducted some meaningful ideas on how to do things differently. I uncovered a new way of relating to each other as human beings. Nobody wants to be lonely, even though many of us are lonelier than we're willing to admit. Maybe this book can help. The first chapter, Loving the World, lays the foundation. Then, I recommend you proceed to the chapter you want to work on first. You can choose between three circles of people in your life: (1) your extended network of friends and acquaintances, (2) your family, or (3) your significant other(s). Or read them all, if you wish. Then, in the final chapter, we'll put it all together. Use my ideas as a guideline, as you see fit.

> *"My body had travelled fast, but my heart took a little longer to arrive"*
>
> Paddington

In addition to this book there are many valuable bonus resources available online, with links to the other books in the Freedom Project series, as well as links to useful websites and additional content. You can find all extra resources through the web page of this book:

www.freedomprojectbook.com

While I was waiting for my flight home today I saw a forty-something year old guy with his girlfriend taking off to some far destination. They seemed independent and dependent at the same time, yet happy to be together. I want to be like them: in a relationship because I want to, not because I have to. I want to be able to leave at all times, but choose not to. That's freedom: freedom to love.

With lots of love for you,

Wilko van de Kamp
Calgary - April 2018

Living a life by experience

When you remove all the noise and distractions, the main reason I love traveling the world boils down to this: to undergo a certain experience. In my Travel book I introduced my concept of Experience Value. It's a model I've used to make sure I get the most out of my travels, regardless of whether I'm on a far-flung city trip, an all-inclusive beach vacation or a luxury business retreat. Travel takes me out of my old familiar comfort zone, and introduces all sorts of interesting experiences I couldn't have had when I stayed at home. One of the reasons that prompted me to write my Happiness book was my desire to take the experience of freedom that I had while I was traveling home with me. Freedom is the ultimate mental souvenir.

When I moved to Canada I never expected to see Paris again. Paris had grown to be my second hometown, and I have a deep appreciation for Gertrude Stein's quote when she says, "America is my country and Paris is my hometown", even though I opted to move to northern neighbor Canada. Canada is my country and Paris my hometown. The "joie de vivre" I experienced in Paris, loosely translated to "joy of living", sums up the essence of that mental souvenir I was longing for. From one Eiffel tower to another, I'm also a frequent Las Vegas visitor. Sin City is a perfect little break from the bitter cold Canadian winters. While I love Vegas, the city is the ultimate showcase of how North America knows everything about entertainment, but little about pleasure. The ultimate take-away for me from that solo visit to Paris was a lifestyle goal. Like the Parisians, I wanted to spend all night wining and dining on a patio with my loved one. I pictured my future partner and I, sipping on a bottle of good wine and enjoying a simple meal. I wanted to enjoy that life at home, drink good wine, and make fresh bread and gourmet meals to enjoy by myself, with my partner or with a small group of true friends. To display my unshakeable commitment to that goal, I bought myself a Parisian wine decanter and wine serving set on that trip. At least, it was a start.

My first trips to Paris were by car. I drove my beat-up, rusty-but-reliable Volkswagen Polo and squeezed as much mileage out of it as I could. They don't make a lot of cars that small in North America, but my faded-red Polo was enough to get me to Paris. Being a working student and very small business owner, on those trips I was on a tight budget. On my first trip back to Paris from Canada thing were quite different. I splurged on a high-end hotel; one I would have never imagined possible on those first budget road trips. Even though Experience Value transcends financial value, I've learned to save and invest my money properly. The money management system I use makes sure I'm in a position to spend a little more money if that allows me to undergo a certain experience. As a result I've been blessed to experience many things I never deemed possible growing up. The memories range from swimming with dolphins to chartering a helicopter to fly over Manhattan, just to get the right angle for a picture I had always wanted to take. While I initially started traveling on a very small student budget, Experience Value also means I'd rather not do certain things while I'm traveling. The experience I might have when I'm staying at a very cheap hotel in a bad neighborhood is not one I'm particularly interested in anymore. On my last trip to Paris, I almost ended up homeless because

I thought I could save a few dollars by booking a hotel on a popular travel website, which ultimately did not turn out in my favor.

The right level of Experience Value directly translates to a higher level of happiness. While I had accomplished that while traveling, my ultimate goal was to bring that lifestyle home. In my Happiness book I write about how I wanted to live every day of my life in a way that allows me to get the maximum Experience Value out of that day. The lifestyle of Living by Experience goes beyond the popular "doing one thing a day that scares you": I wanted to incorporate the guiding principle of Experience Value into my life permanently, on a much deeper level. It's why I do the work I do, and why I started my travel, photography, and lifestyle magazine. Living by Experience shares my story of living the dream and following my passions, not based on any particular model or structure, but by trying out and experiencing different things and seeing what sticks. Please accept my invitation to follow me and join me on my journey:

www.livingbyexperience.com/join

If I can do it, so can you. So the real question is: what are you going to do today that excites you and contributes to the goals in your life? We are here to live by, and for, the experience, and have some fun along the way. Don't take life too seriously.

Bon voyage.

THE WORLD

FREEDOM TO ENJOY NEW EXPERIENCES

Loving The World

Whenever I get gloomy with the state of the world, I think about the arrivals gate at Heathrow Airport. General opinion's starting to make out that we live in a world of hatred and greed, but I don't see that. It seems to me that love is everywhere. Often, it's not particularly dignified or newsworthy, but it's always there - fathers and sons, mothers and daughters, husbands and wives, boyfriends, girlfriends, old friends. When the planes hit the Twin Towers, as far as I know, none of the phone calls from the people on board were messages of hate or revenge - they were all messages of love. If you look for it, I've got a sneaky feeling you'll find that love actually is all around.

Love Actually

My snowboarding adventure

In my collection of mental souvenirs that I brought home from my travels, there are many that equate to a positive Experience Value. My inspiration to share those stories with you comes directly from my travels all over the world. Travel is what keeps me going. I fell in love with all the exceptional things I saw and the many remarkable people who crossed my path. This book however is not about mental travel souvenirs. This book is about my greatest nemesis: love.

The word "love" is used in many different situations. The word is defined as an extreme affection towards someone or something. According to Wikipedia, love is a variety of different emotional and mental states, typically strongly and positively experienced, that ranges from deepest interpersonal affection to simple pleasure. Love means something different to everyone. We can argue about the definition, but reality makes a long story short. My reality is that my failures in love exceed my successes. Then again, that applies to almost all of us these days. Relationships, like friendship, are more and more treated like an exchangeable commodity. Not all experiences will be positive. The negative ones will just give you more contrast to see what you truly want and are passionate about. In this book I'll share some of mine.

Combining my model of maximizing Experience Value with the idea of try-everything-once, I decided to take a trial lesson to try my hand, and feet, at snowboarding. I've been skiing for many years, and it's one of the reasons I moved to Canada. Who wants to spend sixteen hours on a bus to France to go skiing maybe once or twice a year when you can have world-class ski resorts in your backyard? It's one of the advantages of living in the Great White North. Despite my many years of skiing, I had yet to try snowboarding.

Encouraged by the instructor who said I picked up faster than most, I bought myself some brand new snowboarding gear. After my lesson, I had gathered enough courage to venture out to the mountains to practice some more. That's where things went downhill, literally. After some very painful days, I now believe my teacher gives all his students that same encouraging but deceitful line, making them believe they're picking up fast. Either way, I added snowboarding to my list of things I'm not good at in life, and I'm at peace with that.

From a skier's perspective, nobody really seems to know how to practice the opposing art of snowboarding properly anyway. Sliding down the hill on a single edge, like most snowboarders do, doesn't count. That "technique" wipes away all the snow for everybody else, turning the run into an ice rink at best. Chances are that by now I've upset some of my snowboarding readers, so let me add this: True snowboarders know how to make their turns properly. They carve through the snow, leaving the snowpack intact for everybody else's enjoyment. Riding a snowboard that way takes skill. That being

> *"I'd rather be in the mountains thinking of God, than in church thinking about the mountains."*
>
> *John Muir*

said, I've seen very few "wanna-be-cool" snowboarders succeed at executing a proper technique.

Despite my bruised behind following my snowboarding adventure, I still believe you should try most things in life not just once, but at least three times. The first time everything new is awkward. The second time you might think "hmm, interesting". When you persist and make it to the third time, chances are you will start to realize whether you truly like the experience, or not. Maybe you've even picked up some skills along the way. We can only hope. In terms of snowboarding, I sure didn't. I went out with my brand new gear not just three, but at least five times. My "skills" got progressively worse. I also missed my ski's and decided I was much happier on those, despite the much more comfortable snowboard boots. I decided to sell my brand new gear so I'd make my investment back, and someone more fortunate would be able to enjoy my snowboarding equipment more than I did. I felt beyond relieved when my gear was all gone. I took that feeling as proof that I'm really a skier at heart, and fine with it. I don't have to master everything in life, some things are better left to those who enjoy it and are good at it. Besides, who wants to spend a hundred dollars or more on a lift ticket and spend all day sitting on snow?

The whole point of living by experience is to test everything, and keep the things that work. Try everything at least once, and decide after if you want to undergo that experience again. If you do something and you didn't like it, that's not a mistake, it's just an experience. The only mistake would be to seek out that same experience again, now knowing you didn't like it in the first place. The motto behind my Living by Experience magazine is exactly that: living the dream, one at a time.

An alien perspective to the world

We all want to be free. I started the first chapter of my Happiness book with that bold, but undisputed statement. True freedom is an essential ingredient for feeling alive, and comes from the ability to make a choice to do, or not do, something. This book going to press marks the completion of my first decade of living the dream in Canada. Ten years have gone by. Time flies when you're having fun, or not having any fun at all. It's been a hell of a ride, and I'm grateful to those who shared some of that journey with me.

My Canadian love story started back in 2008, I was twenty-six years old at the time: "young, green, and very naive". I knew I didn't want a "normal" life. I wanted something different. Not because the life I had in Europe was so bad. It was pretty great, actually. The ability to just get in my car and drive to Paris is one of the many great perks of living in the hustle and bustle of Western Europe. The endless rain and never ending traffic congestion are a few others. But in deciding to leave all of that comfort and familiarity behind, the reasons that pushed me away from there were not the most compelling ones. It was the reasons that pulled me towards change. My sense of adventure kicked in, and I wanted a change of scenery. Well, if you're looking for scenery, Canada is definitely a place to consider. And I did, amongst a few other places.

For example, I would have loved to build a life in a warm place, close to a beach somewhere. I considered Spain and even South America. Being practical as I am I decided it would be a good idea to speak the language of my new home country fluently before moving there. That limited my options to Dutch and English. My Spanish, French and German were not of the level that I'd be comfortable dealing with everyday practicalities, like calling a plumber or doctor when needed. I watched many documentaries and reality shows about people moving to different countries. It never failed to amaze me how many people move to countries like Spain or France without speaking a single word of the local language. A lot of them decided to begin a bed and breakfast, hotel, restaurant, or otherwise pick up a career in the hospitality industry, without much or any experience in that field. Their interactions with local suppliers and contractors makes for entertaining television. I commend all of them for their courage, but decided a language barrier was not something I was interested in dealing with.

That limited my options to a few countries. Australia didn't make the cut due to their poisonous creepy crawlies. The United States was high on the list but their immigration policies to become a permanent resident appeared to be next to impossible to crack, so I opted for the Northern neighbor Canada as a good second choice. My first exploratory trip to the great white north was in the dead of winter. Many people told me winters get pretty bad, so I figured dealing with the country at its "worst" would be a good test to see if I could make it. If you can make it here in winter, you can make it anywhere.

And I did, with several ups and downs along the way. This book shares some of them. I'm still around. I'm happy I made the move out here in 2008, and also happy I'm still here. Would I do it all again? Honestly, I'm not sure. In terms of relationships, living here has changed everything I believed in and once stood for. If I did get to do it all over again, I would make all the same mistakes once again, just a lot faster. I wouldn't wait as long to see if things would turn out for the better, but make a decision sooner. And that pretty much sums up the past decade: making mistakes, getting knocked down, and trying again.

Three years after moving to Canada, I flew back to Europe for the first time. I wrote in my journal that I was planning to use the upcoming weeks to reflect on the past years, and find an answer on where to go next. Somehow I couldn't do that from my new homeland. I had to use travel as a catalyst, remove myself from the familiar, which was still pretty new to begin with. Creating much needed space is often confused with running away and hiding from problems, but sometimes you need to create a physical distance from the day-to-day life to think things over. Immigrating to a new country uproots your life. You sentence yourself to a lifetime of restlessness. It's an irreversible process. Once you've cut off your roots once, they'll never grow back to the same depths again. At some level, you'll always feel like an outsider, someone who doesn't really belong anywhere anymore.

I arrived in Amsterdam feeling lost, overwhelmed and out of place. It was nice to be home. The familiarities were comforting in a way, but it wasn't home anymore. Part of me wanted to leave the minute I arrived. When I visited my old apartment building, I felt like looking through a window from the outside into a different lifetime. Even though I instantly remembered all the back roads I used to dodge busy traffic on the way to the beach, I felt out of place. I didn't belong there anymore either. Of course my family and friends were welcoming and happy to see me. Despite the welcoming people, I couldn't shake the image of the hopes and dreams I was holding on to when I left three years prior to that trip. Most of it had turned out entirely different than what I had planned for. I had subconsciously, and maybe unwillingly, been upgraded to a "global citizen".

Things had changed so much since I moved to Canada. Even though not everything had worked out the way I planned, everything had been for the better. We worry so much sometimes, especially when the outcome is unknown or uncertain. Life however, starts at the end of your comfort zone. And once you made it into that unfamiliar, or even hostile territory, all you have to do is hold on tight and enjoy the ride. Venturing out into the unknown, far out of my comfort zone, has led to some amazing experiences as well as amazing people, places and things I wouldn't have known had I not taken the plunge into the snow banks of the Great White North. In this first chapter of the book I'll share some colorful examples with you about the beautiful people I've met, the multi-faceted culture I've learned to love, and the massive country I now call home.

> *"In the end, we only regret the chances we didn't take, the relationships we were afraid to have, and the decisions we waited too long to make."*
>
> Unknown

Being a Dutchman in Canada is my version of Sting's song about an Englishman in New York. Let's take that alien perspective to the next level. Imagine you have just arrived on planet earth. Not as a newborn baby, but as a visitor from a foreign, more advanced planet. I'm not sure if extraterrestrial life exists, and exploring the answer to this question could be the potential topic of a future book, but this time it probably won't be. From this imagined alien state, I just watch and observe the world around me. I look at the behavior of the inhabitants, their strange customs, and what they are doing to each other. I sometimes watch their daily news. Some of what you'll see is even more primitive than most animals' behavior. And it is considered normal.

Of course you want to be normal and blend in with your surroundings and everyone in it. Being your unique self is what's advocated in most self-help books. Standing out however is feared and ignored the most. Do you really want to be normal? Normal is just a polite version of the word "boring". Take another look at the world. Disturbed unhappy people, in unhappy relationships are what we collectively call normal. I'd rather stand out.

A few years ago there was a study done, interviewing many people who are were about to die. Australian nurse Bronnie Ware spent too many years doing unfulfilling work. She ended up working in palliative care, caring for patients in the final weeks of their lives. In her book, The Top Five Regrets of the Dying, she recorded the dying epiphanies of the people she worked with. Their main emotion was regret. The regret wasn't for the mistakes they made. The main regret was that they did not live their truth. They didn't live the life they really wanted to live, and instead opted to

> *"Life doesn't owe us anything. We only owe ourselves, to make the most of the life we are living, of the time we have left, and to live in gratitude."*
>
> *Bronnie Ware*

live up to expectations of others. Another big one was the regret they worked too hard. Looking back, people wished they had spent more time with their partner and be part of their children growing up. Most regrets are for the things we did not end up doing. If you only had one day, or one week, left to live, what regret would you have for something you did not end up doing?

Fireworks, resolutions and honesty

I overheard a story recently about a new gym being opened. It's called "Resolutions". It's a special kind of establishment, and only functions as a gym during January. The rest of the year, it turns into a bar, with big flat screen televisions and drink specials served every night. The concept of resolutions is great, but reality tends to keep us honest. We write down our New Years resolutions with the best of intentions. Somewhere along the way, usually by the end of January, most of them are forgotten about, until December comes around yet again. Repeating that cycle over and over again won't get you any closer to your goals.

Nothing in life is one hundred percent guaranteed. The best laid out plans can be overturned by something unexpected in the blink of an eye. The best you can do is learn from the past, not live in the past. You have to move on and keep moving, listening to honest feedback along the way. And speaking of honesty, I'll be the first to admit I don't always play by the rules. There's always that grey area that makes things just a tiny little bit more interesting. Not that I'm advocating breaking the rules, for the record.

Anyone who has ever spent New Years Eve in Amsterdam will know the entire country turns into what sounds like a war zone at the strike of midnight. There's fireworks being set off everywhere by everyone. Even during years of recession, a lot of money is blown up into the sky for some short-lived sparkles. For anyone not used to the ritual it might be an acquired taste, but for insiders it's a pretty sight and explosive way to ring in the New Year.

I live in a different country now, and with that habits and rituals are different. After a decade, I'm still not entirely sure what Canada's official New Years tradition is. Fireworks lit by every house on the street definitely are not one of them. At midnight it's surprisingly quiet, mainly thanks to some law or bylaw against the general public setting off fireworks. Judging by my observations in the past few years I came to the following conclusion: Unless you live outside the city limits, it's not a general practice. And that's where I work the grey area a bit. Since I live on the outskirts of the city, I try to light a sparkly or two at midnight, just to ring in the New Year. My neighbors have grown accustomed to some of my Dutch habits, and most years I've had a small audience with people watching in front of their windows. Occasionally they even invited me in for some New Years bubbly after my sparkly. No harm, no foul.

Except this past year things were different. I had no audience, except one less friendly neighbor who, from his dark unlit porch, called me several names my publisher insisted to not put in writing. "Fire hazard" was one of the lesser offensive things shouted across the fence at midnight. He even threatened to come over "on the count of three". By the tone of his voice the intent of his visit was not to exchange a glass of champagne or share New Years resolutions. The whole tirade was spiced up by a wholesale supply of F-bombs and other allegations that showcased some serious built

> *"Love the life you live, live the life you love"*
>
> *Bob Marley*

up anger management issues. Maybe he didn't get what he wanted for Christmas. It happens, and for that I'm, in true Canadian fashion, very sorry.

Now I'm not denying, or admitting, for legal reasons, any of those allegations. Having made my share of mistakes, I'd be the first to admit I fit the bill on some of the names he called me. He was also right on the fire hazard, probably. Even though it was none of my fault, I once nearly set half the Alberta prairie on fire when a power line on my acreage caught fire, on my birthday. In my defense, neither of those things have much to do with professional fireworks used in a responsible manner. My first hour of the New Year was interesting, even gave a little food for thought, but ultimately prompted me to have another glass of champagne.

I'm giving up on being Mr. Persistence

The New Years story illustrates how our mind works: in dualities. Things are true or false, yes or no, dark or light, good or bad, right or wrong. To organize the world you live in, your mind is designed to pick one, or the other option. This system is hard-wired into your brain. Your reality depends entirely on which side of the fence you choose to be. The dualities of the mind make storing life's experiences in the database of your brain easier. By labeling something the experience gets stored away in the respective filing cabinet for that topic.

With that in mind, let me share another story from my Canadian adventures. As a fine art photographer, I participated in several street markets and festivals. I attended one every weekend, and some people called me Mr. Persistence. I was always one of the first to set up shop in the morning, and one of the last to leave at night when the event was over. I wanted to get the most out of every event I participated in. Persistence became my middle name. I know what I want and I'm not afraid to ask for it directly when needed. Especially for those on the other side of the fence, with a more indecisive nature, this assessment of my character always proved to be true. Our mind does this all the time. It recognizes certain things we're familiar with, and applies labels to make sense of the world.

A label I'm personally less familiar with is the concept of "patience". I know what I want, and that often means I want it now. This eclectic mix of persistence, indecision and impatience is a tricky one. Initially impatience is a great catalyst for persistence. It keeps me going and motivates me to go after the things I want in life. It works particularly well in sales: persistence helps me to keep picking up the phone and to go after that next customer. I do not rest until everyone is satisfied. But when I don't get the results I want right away, the impatience takes over and eventually kills my motivation. Eventually, impatience is the fire department coming in full force to put out the fire of persistence.

> *"Patience, persistence and perspiration make an unbeatable combination for success."*
>
> *Napoleon Hill*

Even though your mind works in dualities, there's no need to consciously label everything. Just be aware of it, and then let it go. Instead of dealing with the messed up love triangle of indecision, persistence, patience (or the lack thereof), I've learned to let it all go, instead choosing to just being me and see what happens next. The law of non-attachment says that sometimes you have to let go of your goals. Set a goal, and then release it. What might appear to the outside world as giving up, with all the negative connotations associated with it, is suddenly not such a bad thing anymore.

The wrong side of the road

Have you ever driven on the "wrong" side of the road as they do in the United Kingdom and some of their subsidiaries like the Bahamas, Jamaica, Australia and a handful of other islands? The traffic pattern follows a similar right versus wrong mental labeling system: left is right, and right is suicide. When working in some northern parts of the United Kingdom I learned that as long as I followed the other traffic and did what they did I'd be scared, but fine. My biggest trouble with driving on the left hand side occurred when there was no other traffic to follow, especially early in the morning on the way to my next client. Traffic circles or "roundabouts" proved to be particularly tricky. Even when I remembered to go about it clockwise instead of counter-clockwise, I forgot the other traffic was coming at me from the right hand side. They should add those "look to the right" signs they have in London to remind pedestrian traffic at crosswalks, to traffic circles too. Having these in place would have saved at least one of my nine lives.

The whole left and right thing is a rather important duality. As a kid I got in trouble at school for being left-handed all the time. It started when I was only four years old. My teacher said it was a handicap. She treated me as mentally disabled. Later I learned this was just a projection of her limited mindset, which reflected poorly on me but had nothing to do with me. Once you get used to a certain way of thinking, that way of thinking becomes the default way of doing things. Nothing changes until you become motivated enough to make a conscious effort to change your perception. Which, in terms of being left handed, I never planned on doing anyway, despite the ongoing abusive remarks throughout most of my junior high school career.

When I was at the dog park the other day, the left and right topic came up again in an entirely different context. A fellow dog walker asked me whether I had trained my dog to walk on the left or right of me. I never had given the topic much thought prior, but somehow my German shepherd ended up on my left hand side. It just naturally happened that way when I first adopted her, and we both seemed to be fine with that arrangement. For the non-dog-people amongst you, let me set some context. When my dog walks on my left, she does her business on that side too. Get the picture? Since she's trained to do that in the grass, which seems to be the preferred location over the middle of the road, I sometimes end up walking on the "wrong" side of the road allowing her to do her business. Also, that position puts me in between her and children as well as adults who aren't always keen to be greeted by my friendly, but big, shepherd dog.

> *"My goal in life is to be a person as good as my dog already thinks I am."*
>
> — Unknown

Much to my surprise, not everyone agreed to the arrangement. And that's putting it nicely. Some people strongly disagree. Canadians tend to stick to the right hand of the road, despite still being a British subsidiary at some level. I've come to known Canadians as a very friendly group of people. They tend to be apologetic even if you are the one bumping into them. Imagine this immigrant's surprise when a runner purposefully bumped into me while walking my dog in the park behind my house. She was visibly upset and yelled at me I was on the "wrong" side of the "road". To my defense, we were on a walking path, not a road. I still don't get the point. One step sideways would have avoided the whole situation. Anticipation to what's happening around you makes life a lot easier. It avoids accidents, too. I'm glad I didn't end up in a similar incident when I got confused driving in the United Kingdom one early morning on my way to work. Even when I did end up on the wrong side of the road in the small British town they didn't got as upset with me as this Canadian runner. In true British tradition, they just laughed at me, while sounding the horn. My dog walking experience must be the new Canadian way.

Celebrating your successes

Amongst the struggles and setbacks in terms of building a life in Canada, there were a great many successes as well. I've even been accused of being a "big spender". I'm guilty as charged: I enjoy flying business class, being driven around in limousines by private drivers and the "suite life" when it comes to checking in to world-class hotels and resorts. I'm also guy who can intensely enjoy the small things in life. But this book is not about bragging or boasting about either of those things. Travel hacking is not that hard, and if I can do it anyone can. I've shared all my secrets in my travel book. Similarly, bragging or boasting your successes on Facebook or social media is not required. It's one of the reasons I disabled my personal Facebook account for a long time. I had enough of being sold to by the next multi network marketer in my friends list. Like everyone else I'm looking for a true connection with my fellow human beings, and to be of value in that relationship. The key point there is to be of value, not bragging about value.

Celebrating success is important, even if it's small baby steps along the way. When I first took myself out of my comfort zone and learned how to travel, I broke my experience down in small stepping-stones. I committed to make the most out of every step along the way, with varying degrees of success. On my Living by Experience blog you can read my stories about being homeless in Paris, as well as getting complimentary high roller access to "sin city" Las Vegas, and everything in between. Celebrating success is about recognizing your own success. This is a habit you can learn to cultivate. I was once asked to put together a list of one hundred successes I had experienced in my life. It wasn't an easy task, until I realized successes don't need to be something big. I challenge you to give this exercise a try for yourself, right now. Put down my book for fifteen minutes or so and write down a list of one hundred successes you can celebrate from your own life thus far. See how far you can get. And just in case you're looking for things to add to your list, here's one you can put in your success journal every day: I'm still breathing. A success is a success, plain and simple. It doesn't have to be something big, but once you learn to cultivate the behavior of celebrating your successes, sooner or later it will be something beyond your wildest dreams.

The point of the exercise is to get into the habit of acknowledging and recognizing your successes in life. Writing a list or keeping a success journal for yourself has nothing to do with bragging or boasting. Celebrate your successes in a way it's the truth for you, regardless of what anyone else might say or think. Keeping a success journal, a written log of your big and small accomplishments, will help you get into the right success mindset. The real challenge is to make success a habit and write down five successes in your journal every night. The goal is to start celebrating your life, regardless of what circumstances you might be facing right now. Recognition is essential to celebrate your wins. Recognizing your successes will allow your mind to experience more of them. Life will get tough sometimes, and if you keep your wins in the forefront of your mind they will help you develop the mindset you need to get through those difficult situations.

Dream stealers and overcoming fear

What's the most inappropriate four-letter F word you know? Here is mine: fear. Fear prevents people from taking action. The definition of fear is much simpler than most people make it sound. Fear is nothing more but anticipation of pain. It's the nemesis of love. Anticipation is part of the future, which is imagined. The future doesn't exist, so the only place fear exists, is in your mind.

Mark Twain said it well: "I've had thousands and thousands of problems in life, most of which have not happened." The key is to act, in spite of fear about perceived problems. Fear is not a stop sign, even if your mind tells you so. Your mind is programmed to keep you safely inside your comfort zone. Don't believe a word you say or a thought you think. Everything you say and think is built on a framework of made up stories filed in your brain. Your mind constructs this framework based on your own experiences and conditioning from the past. Your story is only real for you. You're the one that made it up. Unfortunately the stories that you've conjured up are usually not supportive of your success. The secret to true freedom is allowing those non-supportive stories to fade into the background, and not believing the thoughts you made up. You can change your story, but only if you choose to.

Once you start changing your story and developing a mindset of success, you have embarked on a life-changing journey to allow yourself to dream bigger. It's your moral imperative to dream big, and love with no regrets. Take a minute to think about the goals you've set for your experience in life. Do they make you feel uncomfortable, a little nervous maybe? If your goals don't scare you a little bit they're not big enough, and instead of propelling you to where you want to be they'll keep you exactly where you are today. You have to believe you will achieve the goals you have set for yourself. In my Happiness book I share everything I've learned about setting goals and seeing them manifest. Having big dreams and goals that scare you a little is a crucial ingredient in accomplishing what you set out to do.

> *"I've had thousands and thousands of problems in life, most of which have not happened."*
>
> Mark Twain

Dreams are valuable. If you're not the keeper of your dreams and keep them safe, your dream stealers will come take them away from you. Your dream stealers usually hide somewhere in your environment, often mistaken for a "support" network, made up of your group of extended friends and family. They make it sound like they have the best of intentions in wanting to protect you from failure. The truth is, they don't allow themselves to dream as big as you do.

Your brain is programmed to keep you in your comfort zone and doesn't want you to grow. Your mind is not designed to bring you success. Your mind only has one single, but very natural job, which is to keep your body safe. In order to do so, by default, your mind prefers to think small. It keeps things easy. Your mind likes it when you stay within your comfort zone. Things are cozy and familiar there. I've seen too many budding authors and want-to-be entrepreneurs who started on their journey, but never saw it through to the end. Somewhere along the way their mind finds ways to talk them out of the process. Your mind will do whatever it needs to do to keep you right where you are, in a "normal" state. If you notice your mind talking you out of growing and developing, all you have to do is recognize that natural behavior. You can counteract the negative effects by celebrating your success even more than you already have. The more you do this, the more you'll get in control of your thoughts. All change will initially require you to be uncomfortable. I never wanted to be normal, or boring. Through travel, I committed to get comfortable being uncomfortable. Your thoughts lead to your feelings, and your feelings lead to actions, which ultimately translates into the results you're seeing in your everyday life. Your thoughts and feelings are your inner world. The results are the outer world and create your experience on a day-to-day basis. The actions you take, or not take, are the bridge between your inner and outer world. If you increase your belief system, your confidence, and your self-esteem you can do and accomplish more.

When your mind encounters something new, its default response is "I know that", so it can promptly be filed away, freeing up resources to focus on keeping you safe once again. Immediately following that response learning and growing stops. As a response say, "thank you for sharing" and put it off to the side. Your mind makes feeling uncomfortable a negative thing, but the only time you're learning and growing effectively is when you're uncomfortable. Your comfort zone is highly overrated. I used travel as a catalyst to train myself to become comfortable with unfamiliar and often uncomfortable situations. People are creatures of habit, and developing that trait of being comfortably uncomfortable is done through practice. Your habit is either action or non-action. The key to success is celebrating small successes and taking one step at a time. Whenever you get overwhelmed all you have to do is come back to that basic principle of celebrating small victories and taking one step at a time.

Developing your goals and dreams, and protecting them from your dream stealers will automatically increase your level of self-consciousness. You'll get more clarity on what you want in your life, and learn to witness your own internal thought processes that tend to talk you out of the goals that are most important to your personal growth. Do yourself a favor and don't let that happen to you. Your life goals are too important to be neglected and ignored any longer.

Feed your curiosity

The default-operating mode is not action, but in-action. When did we all collectively fall asleep and stopped thinking for ourselves? Are we just blindly following warning signs and labels on autopilot, more or less safe-guarded by the beacons of common sense, or lack thereof, on either side of the road we're on? It's a mundane example, but the patio chairs I bought last summer came with a warning label that indicated they could only be used to sit on. There were images depicting forbidden behaviors such as standing or climbing on the chairs. I always wonder if those warning labels are added to the manufacturing process before or after someone attempted to do what is now depicted as a "thou shalt not". Common sense appears to be all but common. But regardless of common sense, when we burn ourselves with hot coffee, which is supposed to be hot, or kill our beloved family pet in an attempt to "dry" it in the microwave, we drag the provider of respectively coffees and microwaves to court. After all, they didn't warn us, and because of that they're at fault for that in-action. As a result of that litigation my coffee comes with a label that says, "Careful, the beverage you're about to enjoy is extremely hot", even in cases where that's not true.

David Chilton, better known as the Wealthy Barber, said:

"The most commonly seen characteristic of happy people: They're curious. They love to read, they love to travel, and they love to listen to other people's opinions. In short: they love to learn! If you

can teach your kids one thing, I think it will lead to happiness, is to develop curiosity."

A healthy dose of self-consciousness is beneficial, but don't become too self-conscious. When you do, you may end up avoiding talking to groups of people, or even individuals. Make it a habit to openly approach groups of people and introduce yourself to them. Ask genuine questions about other people, and show an authentic interest in their answers. Listen carefully and attentively to what people say and respond to show your interest. Interacting with people will make you feel less lonely, and more relaxed about your own goals. You will find it easier thank you think to speak to groups of people. By concentrating on what others are saying, you'll find time to relax instead of being too consumed with yourself and getting your own goals and ideas across. Relax into it and it'll naturally happen.

> *"I have learned that there is more power in a good strong hug than in a thousand meaningful words."*
>
> Ann Hood

I attended a conference a few months before this book was published where we started every morning with giving each other "heart-to-heart" hugs. After about two days of that, many participants, myself included, broke down in tears. We realized how much we had craved that missing, true connection with others. In our Western society our DNA is deprived of the feeling of being surrounded by loving, supporting people who care for you. We're afraid of missing out. Things change constantly. Names of people will change. The technology we use will change. But people never change themselves. The issues we face today are the same we faced all along. Our basic instincts and desires have existed for thousands of years, and will continue to exist for thousands more. Our desires are hard-wired into our genetics. The top three general desires revolve around food, love, and money. Once you know that, you can appeal to it and engage with people on a deeper level. Your story will change from pushing your own ideas to being of service, and developing a genuine interest in helping others.

Love and opportunity where you are

Once you become your true self, and represent yourself that way towards the outside world, people will automatically and naturally connect with your authenticity. As part of that connection, you'll undoubtedly get their feedback, which can either be positive or negative. Always look at what feedback you're getting. Especially when things don't seem to work out the way you had envisioned, feedback is a valuable tool. Use feedback to refocus and get clarity. Be honest with yourself answering some questions about the goal you're after. Why is there a real or perceived roadblock in your way?

Reflection doesn't mean giving up on your goals. Neither does asking difficult questions. It's an attempt to find a way around the roadblock or turn it into a stepping-stone. Chances are that thanks to that roadblock, you might never reach your original goal, but an even bigger one instead. The setback might make you question the goal, give you an opportunity to revisit the original goal, and optionally make it bigger, better, or different altogether. Or maybe you'll recommit to it but go about after accomplishing your goal in a different way. The results always look better later. You won't realize the lessons learned until after the fact, which doesn't negate the fact that some experiences in life are painful and seemingly impossible to deal with.

In every negative event lies an equal or bigger opportunity. That might be hard to see at first, but if I think back to any negative event that has happened in my life, they've all turned out for the better in the end. I didn't see any of that at the time. One of the bravest things I've done in my life is continue living when I didn't see the light at the tunnel anymore. But I instinctively knew the light had to be there somewhere, even if my clouded mind didn't see it at the time. I'm glad I did or you wouldn't be holding this book today. And I would have missed out on the life I enjoy living today. It's always easier to spot those lessons well after the fact, once you've already earned the things you needed to learn from them. A lot of our accomplishments in life aren't recognized until after the fact. On the way there I had no idea some of those experiences were going to be an accomplishment. As Robert Frost said, "the best way out is always through".

Today, I try to remember one question when something happens to me that I regard as negative: "What opportunity is this?" I'm not at all perfect at it, and being impatient as I am I still can get quite worked up when something doesn't appear to be working out the way I had envisioned. There's a real world truth in asking yourself this profound question. Even if you don't have the answer, asking the question helps you to start recognizing opportunities where you didn't think there were any. A gift resides in every moment. Hidden in every negative event is an equal or bigger opportunity. Like a tiny mustard seed, which over time can grow into something bigger. It's up to you what are you going to do with that opportunity. How are you going to respond to the next event you think is negative, to find the seed of opportunity hidden in there? While you might not be able to control most of your circumstances, looking for opportunities is a choice you can make every day.

Let go of some people

I've often ignored negative feedback because it made me feel bad. After I moved to Canada, it took me years of trying to get over the negative feedback from my family. They didn't like or supported my departure. There's a whole chapter in this book dedicated to the topic of family. Where do those negative emotions come from? We feel bad because we're addicted. We're addicted to approval from others. Like true addicts, we stay within the comfort zone of getting our "fix". When the high wears off we go back for more. We're preprogrammed to constantly seek and obtain external approval. Especially when important life choices are involved, the external approval is necessary for most. Instead of inquiring within, we place a higher value on other people's perceptions and ideas. We look at our extended network, our friends, family, and loved ones. We're not looking for support from them in living our dreams, but we're looking for guidance as to what to do next. We're hungry for clues to reveal the hidden expectations they might hold for us, trying to fulfill them. In exchange we get another small dose of approval, keeping us within our comfort zone. But you never looked inside, asked yourself what you wanted to do. No wonder so many people feel unfilled, not just in the work they're doing but in the life they're living. By not looking inside and asking the one person that matters where to find true fulfillment, you will forever prevent yourself from reaching your life's true potential.

Before doing anything else, let's go through an approval detox. Learn to spend less time building the wrong relationships. The wrong relationships can be as toxic as the wrong food. This might mean you have to let go of some people and quit the mediocre club. It's not an easy process. My Happiness book shares the path I've followed to do this for my career and business life. The process is similar but gets much harder when you're applying it to your personal life. People get involved, as well as emotions and some real feelings and beliefs we hold about others and ourselves. Following my dream, I took the plunge and moved to North America, despite of my family's ongoing objections and accusations. The physical separation didn't make the process easier, but this book is about love, not about easy. Addicts will run from the pain, instead of moving towards it. I felt the pain, for years, and decided to move through it regardless.

> *"Success is not final, failure is not fatal: it is the courage to continue that counts."*
>
> Winston Churchill

Two things helped me move forward, and eventually through those difficult times of letting go of my approval addiction: goals, and failures. I truly believed I could achieve each of the goals I had set for myself. That belief wasn't always a bright shining light. At times it was reduced to a flickering candle at best. By taking the next step in faith, I acted as if my goals had already come true. Not everything worked out the way I planned. So, in addition to my goals I also embraced failure, but I didn't recognize failure. Henry Ford didn't recognize failure, even though he went bankrupt twice. Champions keep their momentum going until they get to the end result. Your psychological momentum always moves faster than your physical momentum, so work on the mind first. Choose your thoughts wisely, and reality will follow.

Every thought and feeling you have, you'll bring with you to every action you take and interaction you have. In moving to Canada, I left everything and everyone familiar behind, but I took the one thing with me that I could not leave behind: myself. You carry your emotions into any relationship you're in, which will impact the results you're seeing. If a relationship is full of negative emotions like sadness, fear, anger, shame, guilt or even a basic worry about any of those topics, those emotions will influence that relationship. They will drag the relationship and the people within it down as if you had been thrown in New York's Hudson River with your feet in a block of concrete.

We're conditioned to look for what's wrong in everything we see and exprience in life. Chances are you immediately noticed the typo in the previous sentence, before even attempting to comprehend what I was trying to say. Your mind immediately focused on what's wrong. Instead, recondition your mind to look for the positive and learn to celebrate the wins. Find and focus on positive, supportive emotions in the relationships you have with others. What applies for relationships, applies for opportunities as well. Once bring your emotions, good or bad, into an opportunity, you'll find it's not the same opportunity anymore. Before doing anything, you've already altered your reality based on the thoughts and emotions you brought to the table with you. Without looking at what's actually in front of you, your mind has already started to disqualify the opportunity. Your mind doesn't like change, or growth. It wants to keep you safe, and knock anything unfamiliar off the table. Knowing that, it's imperative to clear your dark clouds so they will not impact your future any longer. Negative emotions are nothing more but stuck energy, waiting to be released.

What are you filling your mind with? It's your life. You're the author of your own story, and it's your birthright to make that story a best-seller. Ultimately your thoughts are what define you. The thing that connects us all is the beliefs we hold about ourselves. You have the gift to believe in yourself. In my darkest days I realized I had a choice. I could continue to copy my past behaviors and hold on to the values that other people had about me, or instead start believing in myself. Looking for approval from others in our deepest, darkest moments instead of believing in ourselves is not conducive to anything positive, especially the freedom, happiness and love you're after. Make a choice for yourself instead of going back to your drug dealer time and time again for another dose of approval. With a healthy level of self-confidence, dare to cheer for yourself, and learn to believe in yourself. Deep at the bottom of that well of darkness and loneliness you'll find your truest, most authentic self.

YOUR NETWORK

OPENING UP TO THE PEOPLE AROUND YOU

Loving Your Network

Gandhi said that whatever you do in life will be insignificant, but it's very important that you do it. Because nobody else will. Like when someone comes into your life and half of you says you're nowhere near ready, but the other half says: make her yours forever.

Remember me

Living the Pura Vida

Meet Tim, a thirty-five year old executive at a high-pressure investment firm. Tim has at all; a big home just outside of the city, a beautiful and supportive wife, two healthy kids, and last but not least a five-car garage including a vintage red Porsche sports car. Tim says he's living the dream. To support his family, he works at least sixty hours per week. Occasionally he even breaks the seventy-hour mark. Even on vacation, Tim often slips away from the rest of the family to go online in the hotel lobby, check his emails, messages and answer missed phone calls from important clients. He sees nothing abnormal about his behavior. Everyone at his office works like that. "It's the price you pay for success", he says.

In North America, we overvalue the idea of busyness, and undervalue time. North Americans work longer hours than people in any other industrialized nation. In Europe, North America is viewed as a "nation of workaholics". According to a report from the United Nations International Labor Organization (ILO), "Workers in the United States are putting in more hours than anyone else in the industrialized world." I clearly didn't read that memo before making my transatlantic move, and in true Living by Experience fashion, I opted to learn the lesson the hard way.

What are we working those long days and weeks for? Even though I wrote a best selling book about travel, it's not extravagant vacations we put in all the extra hours for. The typical American worker has an average of only two weeks of vacation as compared to four to six weeks for their European counterparts. That alone might be the reason why I never found my permanent place in corporate Canada. How is it that anyone is remotely ok with the idea of only getting back ten days of their time every year to do what they want? Asking another human being for my own time back, whether paid or unpaid, is an outrage, and inappropriate form of modern day slavery. Another lesson I learned the hard way after my transatlantic relocation.

Do we work for happiness then? I wrote an entire book in this series about Happiness at work. According to regular surveys by the National Opinion Research Center of the University of Chicago, no more Americans report they are "very happy" now than in 1957, despite almost doubling our personal consumption expenses. The world's population has consumed as many goods and services since 1950 as all-previous generations combined, but it doesn't make us any happier. Since then, times have changed, but our core human issues have stayed exactly the same. The majority of people continue to be unhappy about the work they're doing. We're still struggling with love, happiness and freedom just as much now as we were at any point in history. Just the circumstances have changed.

There are serious costs to working so hard. Most heart attacks in the United States happen between 4am and 10am on Monday mornings. Heart attacks occurring between 6 a.m. and noon are also considered to be more severe. During the rest of the week, we tend to cut back on sleep and time with our families. Almost a third of people working more than forty-eight hours a week said that their permanent state of exhaustion was affecting their relationships, including their married life. Nearly a third admitted that work-related tiredness was causing their sex life to suffer, with a reduced or completely lost sex drive. They also complained that long hours at work and frequent required overtime led to arguments and tension at home. Most of them blamed the long hours as a direct cause of their disagreements. To make matters worse, they felt guilty for not pulling their weight with domestic chores. Sounds familiar? Guilt and resentment are always linked, and founded in the same negative emotion. It's your choice whether to maintain the status quo or challenge the limiting belief by taking action before it's too late.

Despite popular belief, struggling financially and not having time with your kids, family and loved ones is not how life has to be. There's no need to choose between living a fulfilled life and financial stability of a regular day job. Admitted, as an "independent", my schedule is different from most corporate employees, and my income tends to fluctuate a bit. But ultimately, the journey has been worth it. The idea that you can't have both might be a conspiracy between employers, attempting to prolong our modern day slavery for as long as they can. Looking back, building an independent career worked out way better than you ever would have been able to describe to me when I first started out. But first, I had to learn stop living for the weekend.

On one of my trips I discovered Costa Rica and it's lifestyle of "Pura Vida", which translates to enjoying life and taking your time to celebrate it. To some, Pura Vida is also known as the opposite of what we're doing in the west. We're always in a rush and never really taking our time to do anything, let alone "celebrating life". I found Costa Rica to be an eclectic mix of local, North American, European and even

Argentinean cultures. The people are very friendly, always helpful, but best of all laid-back. Costa Rica is becoming more and more popular with people looking to permanently move there, in an attempt to get away from all the undesired side effects the hustle and bustle of Western Life includes. If you've been to Costa Rica, or even looked at some of my travel photography from Central America, it's easy to see why so many people are falling in love with the country. If you've ever dreamed of getting away from it all, Costa Rica could be your answer.

> *"The cure for anything is salt water: sweat, tears or the sea."*
>
> Isak Dinesen

Even for most workaholics, the worst day at the beach is still better than the best day in the office.

How do you know if workaholic habits have snuck too far into your daily routines? It doesn't matter whether you have a regular job, or work for yourself. Even though I was working independently at the time, I saw all the warning signs of being a workaholic. But, like a true addict, I was in deep denial about all of them.

For starters, my entire home was organized just like another office. Work was everywhere you looked. I enjoyed taking time off to travel, but I kept my cell phone and laptop in close proximity at all other times. Travel and vacations were the only exception where I chose to truly disconnect and enjoy myself and the people I was spending quality time with. Regardless of disconnecting physically, work problems kept circling in my mind, even during my precious time off. To make matters worse, I slept only a few hours each night as sleeping seemed like a waste of time. Time is money, I told myself.

I lost a few friends during this time. They didn't bother calling me anymore, or when they did I'd find an excuse to get off the phone quickly. People who loved me complained about the many hours I spent in my office or working on my projects. Sometimes they went as far as begging me to take some time to myself. Meanwhile, success at work made me happier than any other aspect of my life at that time. Most of my colleagues described me as hard working, needing to win, and some would even argue I was overly committed.

If you recognize some of these warning signs on a regular basis, it may be time to re-evaluate how you are handling the priority of work in your life. Don't wait until it's too late. A balanced and healthy life includes quality time dedicated to your loved one and family. Love, in any form, takes time and commitment. Don't be so busy making a living that you forget to make a life.

Temptation: there's only one way to find out

I get bored easily, and to stay busy I'm always doing a variety of different things I enjoy. Anything that's outside of the limitations of a job description is where the real fun begins. A job is like a comfort zone: the things you want in life are outside of that comfort zone. The grass is always greener on the other side of the fence. The same applies to love and relationships. Instead of choosing for freedom, people place restrictions on the other party in the relationship. It's not for no reason that significant others are perceived and talked about as the old ball-and-chain. It might be a stereotype, but the one thing I've learned from my travels is that all stereotypes hold a certain degree of truth.

The beauty, or problem, with temptation is that you'll never find out, unless you give in. Which seems to be a bad thing usually. Just like the old ball-and-chain, temptation also has a bit of a bad name. "Thou shalt not" do a whole bunch of tempting things. You'll never know how far you can go, if you're not willing to risk going too far. If you don't like the outcome, it's always possible to revise a decision and take a few steps back onto the beaten path. That lifestyle requires an open mind from all parties involved. The reason so many relationships fail, both professional and personal alike, might well be the lack of freedom we allow the other person to enjoy, leaving ourselves stuck with an unfilled "what if" somewhere in the back of our mind. Most regrets are for things we did not end up doing.

I used to have my own art gallery, a physical retail location where I was selling my photographic art. Even though I almost exclusively work the online fine arts space today, running a physical store was a great experience. I consider it one of the highlights of my creative career thus far. The location, a business revitalization zone on the edge of downtown Calgary, wasn't perfect, which made it all the more interesting. People weren't used to finding art on their street, and I often saw them walking back and forth in front of my big gallery windows, unsure whether they would risk entering or not. They were curious, tempted even. Some gave in, others didn't. A few of the ones that didn't come in literally walked away backwards. One or two almost tripped over the A-frame sign I had strategically placed on the sidewalk. They went through all that trouble resisting their curiosity to see something they hadn't experienced before. Today, they're probably still stuck on fighting the temptation to experience something they hadn't seen on their street before. I've moved on from that location since, so in the end we'll never know what might have happened.

Looking back, the art gallery story made me wonder about people's thought process. Maybe they figured I was some shady car salesman that wouldn't let them leave my "showroom" ever again until they signed their life away to buy a piece of my art. It's certainly possible they thought that way. But in retrospect I'm sad some of them didn't come in. Maybe I should have held the door open to make it easier. There's only one way to find out and learn something new: jumping in. Marcel Proust said we don't receive wisdom. You'll have to figure it out on your own by saying "yes", and learning from every experience life throws at us. Open your mind or someone will open it for you.

Life is just like an Etch a Sketch. Just as you think you got your life figured out, someone comes by or something happens which shakes the thing up and makes you start all over again. After my art gallery days, I was committed to add something new. Even though I didn't abandon my arts career at all, I wanted to add something different to the mix. Wanting to share some more stories from my art gallery experiences, as well as the inspiration behind my artworks, I was playing with the idea of starting a blog about my journey of building a creative career. I hesitated: what if it all failed? I might make a fool out of myself by writing down what I'm trying to do. I didn't consider myself successful at this time and was merely trying to get by. I was sure all the established industry experts would see my upcoming failure coming from the start, of course without saying anything or offering useful advice to save me. It was my worst nightmare. They would just sit there and watch me suffer, maybe even laugh a little or write about me on their own blogs.

> "I have not failed. I've just found ten thousand ways that won't work."
>
> *Thomas Edison*

In a way we all fail. Real courage is in the trying. So I decided to give it a shot anyway. Both the artistic career and writing about my journey on my blog. The idea behind that blog eventually turned into the bestselling book series you're holding today. My original blog turned into the Living by Experience magazine and has grown way bigger than I anticipated when I first contemplated the idea of writing down some of my experiences and experiments. More importantly, writing turned out to have some real therapeutic qualities. In one way, the blog gave me a platform to "revenge" the many setbacks and struggles on my journey by writing about them publicly. Overcoming hurdles has become easier simply by writing about them and sharing my experiences. Even if something doesn't work out, I'm now just being grateful for another topic to write about, and carry on with my day. It might benefit someone else. I've finally mastered looking for that equal or bigger opportunity, even in negative events. Success is about progress, not perfection.

Latte Art

Years ago I said that I would probably be a terrible coffee shop owner. Just like I used to do with photo sessions when I first started as a photographer, I keep giving coffee away for free. Maybe it's a Dutch thing. Whenever I hire someone to do some work around the house for me, I give them coffee, for free. And I don't brew the cheap stuff. Whether you're here to clean, paint, or build a deck or fence; my espresso machine grinds the beans for a fresh cup of coffee every time. And, needless to say, on top of the free coffee I pay my contractors too. Giving out free coffee is just the right thing to do in my caffeinated Dutch mind.

Many independent coffee shops feature local artists, and as a photographic artist I'm always looking for places to display my work. By now, my work has been featured in a fair share of local, independent cafes. Not to sound ungrateful, because I truly appreciate the wall space in local businesses to showcase my work, but none of the coffee shop owners I worked with ever offered me a single cup of coffee. I'm a cheap date and don't fancy sugary lattes. Just a black cup of coffee would have been nice from time to time while I was working up a sweat decorating their store walls free of charge. I usually show my work a month at a time and aim to visit regularly during that month, buying at least a cup of coffee every time, and usually something to eat. I always bring in friends and schedule business meetings at whatever place is currently featuring my work. The coffee shop owner gets extra business, and free high quality artwork for their walls. In return I might get some good exposure, but no coffee. And exposure alone doesn't pay the bills, or my coffees.

Contrary to the small independent shops, large corporate coffee chains don't have local artists in their cafes. They get mass-produced pictures of coffee beans and other coffee related artifacts for their walls. While these cafes won't display my work, they have community boards and are happy to support their local communities by displaying posters of my art events and book releases. Imagine my surprise when one of the store managers saw me hanging a poster for an upcoming gallery reception, and asked whether we needed coffee for the event. They kept their promise and provided me with fresh high quality coffee, as well as all the cups and condiments we needed for the many people in attendance that night. Other than their cups with their logo at my event they didn't get anything out of that deal but to support their community.

And that's what it's all about: support. Most business owners work in the solitary confinement of their office, or from the kitchen table. The old idea of networking isn't based on an artist centric economy where people share something from their passion. With feelings of depression and people feeling miserable at work on the rise, we're heading back to an arts based society where people create and share what they love to the benefit of others. Instead of buying from large corporations, we're dealing with individual creators. Thanks to the power of the Internet these artisans now have the power to operate on a global scale. For the first time they stand a chance to make a living on their own competing with large corporations instead of participating as part of them. It's why I love doing the work I do, even though I have trouble coming up with an exact job title for what I do. While our society is shifting, our way of networking is not yet following suit. I still receive blanket emails from recruiters who use the shotgun approach to finding candidates for their roles. Most of them are fishing from the same pond, and often I receive several emails from different recruiters for the same job opening. No one is attempting to even address me by my name in that email, they just copy and paste the same job description over and over again, hoping someone is desperate enough for a paycheque to respond. I guess for some the model still works, for now, but not for me. Networking can no longer be about what I can do for you as a one-way recipient. Networking is about forming a two-way relationship, a give and take. Many businesses fail and continue to fail because they're treating the relationship with their employees as a one-way model. Cutting people a paycheque is not enough to classify as a two-way street. It has to be about alignment of goals where everybody gets something out of the deal. When that balance is out, either one of the parties suffers. With most fulltime employees being relatively replaceable, it's indeed often those employees who suffer the most. As a result they feel unfulfilled at work, and check out either emotionally and underperform, or physically to go do something different. Until the professional world catches on with the new networking, things will be out of sync for a while. On a small scale, you can start to change the way you network. Think about what you do and offer as a way of being of service: how can you help as

> "Small business people are people with goals and values that can't be calculated on a profit and loss statement."
>
> Linda McMahon

many people as possible and be of value to your network? Conversely, when you're looking to hire someone or buy something, consider your own direct network first. Chances are someone is making some product, or offering their expertise that can be of immediate value to you. The new networking isn't just about the traditional exchange of give and take, but changes the perspective to support. Networking is about being supportive whilst being supported.

Why I don't believe in job security

I've been able to build a large support team for some of my projects, and always attempted to steer clear from micromanaging people. I never wanted to be the type of leader that I hated most. Yet everyone seems to have a career goal of being "the boss". In building my teams, the one thing most candidates mention as one of their career aspirations is to get into a leadership, or management role. I always ask them: Why? What is it about the art of leadership that makes it a goal set by virtually everyone?

Do a quick online search on leadership and you'll find a plethora of leadership books, courses, conferences and programs, containing a never-ending combination of theories about "true" leadership. They all claim to uncover the absolute truth and ultimate key to leadership success. True leadership is claimed by many, defined by a few, and perfected by only a handful unsung heroes. We think we know a lot about leadership, but it is the application of leadership that defines a true leader. The secret sauce of true leadership is that it's an individual concept. Being a leader is exercised in many diverse, yet successful ways. Indeed, success in any form always equates to perceived leadership. This is one of the key principles I teach my authors in my Write a Book in a Week program. I help my clients leverage the power of a published book to grow their business or career, applying leadership principles strategically to grow the level of authority in their field. The opposite holds true as well. Unsuccessful application of leadership skills is without exception counter-productive. Encountering the unsuccessful application of leadership in many parts of my corporate career was one of the main reasons for me to write my book about happiness at work. Even when you're working independently, inexperienced micromanagers pop up where you least expect them. Is what I teach another theory, promising you golden mountains and unbounded success? No, sorry. Instead, I share my observations about where to look for true leadership. It's not about defining true leadership, but about recognizing it when you see it.

Natural leaders exercise leadership regardless of what they're doing. That includes positions not formally designated for leadership. It's those individuals that are often causing problems for the organization they work for. The informal leader creates all sorts of problems for their "official" leadership as defined by the company's organizational chart. In my work as a business and management consultant, I often see this behavior in groups that try to address problems in their work environment. If no one specifically is in charge or takes ownership of a new initiative, the unofficial leader who emerges is often the person who demonstrates the most passion about the topic. The group tends to gather behind the "visionary". This type of leader is passionate about achievements for the community as a whole, but often not about their own individual advancement. These leaders are typically not publicly recognized, because they don't blow their own horns. They are too busy working toward meaningful goals to be distracted by something as counter-productive as public recognition.

Leaders who are passionate about their vision are determined to make sure everyone in the organization knows what that vision is, and gets on board with their idea. Passionate leaders always have a clear vision. In the end, what they accomplished is no longer just a vision, but becomes a tangible part of the environment. Everything that happens is a reflection of that vision, which becomes the beacon that guides everyone in the organization.

Those leaders know their people well: their personalities, their histories, and their passions. A true leader attracts and retains the right people to "get the job done." They implement the theory of W. Edwards Deming. I've taught about Deming's ideas ad nauseam in my service management class. In short, his theory ensures continuous reflection and improvement. If the right people are in the job and they are given the resources to get the job done, cheerleading is a waste of time, because these people already get out of bed in the morning excited about going to work. If you're in a leadership position, please do your team members a favor and read that paragraph again, because most North American managers I've encountered so far would miss the key point entirely: intrinsic motivation. Your team is getting out of bed because they want to, not because they have to. If you feel the need to micromanage your team it's either a reflection of your own insecurity or incapability to do the job, or you have a problem at your hiring level where you've brought people onboard who lack the motivation they need to do their job. The good news is that all of those scenarios are fixable.

> *"Great things in business are never done by one person. They're done by a team of people."*
>
> Steve Jobs

Where do you go to find and cultivate intrinsic motivation within yourself or within your team? It starts with recognizing the benefits of having different personalities around you. Many books and theories are written about building a successful team, and all of them speak about combining different personality traits. Different people bring different approaches, and each of them individually needs to be instrumental to your team's success.

Surround yourself with the right people for the job you need done. Finding the right people is about personality and mindset. The skills you can train. Adequate tools to do the job you can provide. Once you've hired the right people, get out of their way. When a team member is truly motivated, they don't need fancy slogans or mantras to make them behave like a good corporate citizen. They also don't need weekly or even daily meetings to collectively cheer about company events that are already in the past. The "self-actualized" person is also self-motivated. They know their jobs, they know what's expected of them, and they know that they have a responsibility to the rest of the team to do the best job they possibly can. Two universal rules apply to building an intrinsically motivated team. Firstly, any team not performing to this universal standard has a problem at their hiring level. Secondly, any residual form of micromanagement is a sign of lack of experience of the leadership involved. Micromanagers either don't hire the right people or they are they ones that shouldn't have been hired, masking their own insecurity and inability. Focus on bringing in team members with the right mindset, instead of micromanaging the execution and operations level. If you must micromanage them, you don't need them. Or maybe they don't need you.

When true leaders develop this kind of intrinsic motivation within their team, they are freed up to do the visionary work and create the environment for everybody else to succeed. This allows them to stay focused on strategic goals, instead of getting distracted with tactical involvement. Leaders should not need to be directly engaged in the daily operations., but consult feedback to ensure things are working as expected. Feedback helps you assess when to make appropriate changes. Leaders focus their energy on keeping the goal in sight, whilst simply making course corrections when changing conditions require them. From a management perspective this approach means you're constantly working yourself out of a job. Anyone who has ever worked with me in the past has heard me use this sentence at least once. I don't believe in job security. I believe in the opposite of job security. Your main objective is to constantly remove yourself from the equation as much as possible, and at the same time know and acknowledge when you have exceeded your limitations. Get help from a coach or mentor to overcome your obstacles. The right coach will get you results faster than you might be able to do on your own. Recognize that the mind that has created a particular problem in your environment typically cannot resolve that same problem on it's own.

There's also good news for everyone I've interviewed so far: each of you has the capability to be a leader. To become effective leaders, we must dare to be our true self, lose our fear of making mistakes, and share responsibility for achieving common goals. If those goals align with our individual measures of achievement, then the organization will continue to succeed, grow, and achieve remarkable things. If they are not, you will be nothing more but the transient leader that maybe got things going, but never saw it through all the way to the finish line.

Entering voluntary solitary confinement

About a year before this book went to press I visited the beautiful city of San Francisco. As a first time visitor, the mandatory boat trip to infamous prison island Alcatraz had to be on the itinerary. Voluntarily, I spent a few minutes in solitary confinement in a completely dark prison cell. When the door slammed shut behind me I realized I didn't ask how long exactly this experience was going to take. The walls and doors were so thick I couldn't hear or see anything. Even though I knew my confinement would only last a few minutes at most, a slight panic set in and I could tell my heart rate picked up a little. I was happy to be released into freedom shortly thereafter. Imagine having to be in there for days, weeks, or even months on end. The worst punishment within the prison environment they can give an inmate is solitary confinement. Being in prison you already lost your freedom, and given the title of this book series you'll appreciate freedom is one of the things I value most. People can lose their freedom to all sorts of things; whether it's a career, relationship, addiction, or an actual life of crime, which might end you behind physical bars. Solitary confinement takes losing your freedom to a whole other level, and many of the Alcatraz inmates lost their sanity inside those dark cellblocks.

Most entrepreneurs today are "solopreneurs". Unfortunately, most solopreneurs have put themselves into voluntary solitary confinement. They've stripped themselves of their humanity in an attempt to do everything on their own without truly connecting with their fellow human beings. I've been depressed and burned out more than once, but I'd rather be burned out doing something I love than faded out doing something I hate. Still, I was starting to lose my sanity within the solitary confinement of the very business I had created. Set yourself free from the prison of your business. A lot more is possible for you, but you don't have to do it all on your own. Get in the habit of connecting with other people.

I hate seeing people give up on their dream because they get stuck in solitary confinement. They write long to-do lists everyday, but fail to realize writing lists has nothing to do with productivity and achieving results. You might be on your way, but movement does not equal achievement, yet. Focus on outcomes instead of busyness and activities. To get unstuck and break free from the old thinking patterns, you'll need leverage. Aristotle said, "Give me a lever long enough and I'll lift the world". Anything can be accomplished with the right leverage. Connecting with other people will increase your leverage exponentially as you no longer have to do everything on your own all the time. And often overlooked, one of the people you need to connect with more is yourself.

Answering the phone

In the beginning of this book I introduced you to the regrets people have at the end of their life. A lot of those regrets are about not going after their life's goals and dreams. Those are often things that we do, or in this case, did not do. In addition to not fulfilling more desires, another common regret is not having the courage to express true feelings. People suppress their feelings to keep peace with others in their lives. They've designed their lives around expectations from friends, family, and loved ones. We settle for a mediocre life in a failed attempt to please others. We never become who we truly can become, because we're afraid of disappointing someone else in our environment. We're afraid to not live up to their expectations, whether real or perceived. Science has linked many illnesses to the bitterness and resentment people carried as a result of not living their life to the fullest extent possible. In hindsight you always have perfect vision.

Hand in hand with not expressing our truest feelings goes the regret of losing touch with old friends. Often we realize the true value of people until they're long gone from our life. You don't realize what you've got until it's gone, and that applies to more than only romantic relationships. Even though staying in touch is much easier thanks to the Internet, many people lose that true human connection. A while back I had to train one of our newest staff members on properly answering our company phone. She answered with an abrupt "what's up". It wasn't the way I envisioned our phones being answered. Admitted, my first job was in a call center, and people say I sound too professional even when answering my personal cell phone. Either way, it never dawned on me that explaining how to properly answer the phone with your name, the company name and a friendly "good morning" would require any explanation, especially to someone who appeared to be on her phone all the time. Never assume anything. We're always connected; yet feel more lonely and disconnected than ever before thanks to the isolating effect of "social" media.

Everyone misses their friends from the past when they're dying. It's the stories and memories we carry with us. True friendship can be something deeper than the best of romantic relationships. In a friendship, there's less set expectations. A friend leaves more freedom to be your unique self. We don't keep our thoughts and feelings inside as much. It's great to be able to share our accomplishments and disappointments with someone we trust. In a relationship, sharing your deepest thoughts and secrets is often an obligation, which stems from either your own guilt or your partner's pressure. In a friendship, it's not about compromise, and sharing is something you do voluntarily. Friendship is more genuine, which makes us more likely to share directly from the heart, instead of worrying about being the perfect partner. In a friendship, sharing is never a mandatory duty.

Meeting a fellow human being is a precious opportunity to establish a connection. Every moment contains an inherent invitation to connect with the world around you. In connecting with others we can come together to expand our mutual consciousness. We're here to connect with and learn from one another. This holds particularly true for friendship, but it applies to any meeting of the minds. No meeting, or relationship, is pure coincidence. As a generation we've become unfamiliar with making that connection. Like my team member answering the phone, we don't quite know what to say, or how to act. We feel out of place, and in any socially awkward situation staring down to your smart device has become the go-to response. If you're willing to rule out pure coincidence, dare to ask yourself the question why that person is beside you on the plane next time you travel. Ask why someone is in line in front, or behind you, at your favorite coffee shop. Even better: ask them a question. People are waiting to be connected with. They might not know how to take that first step. We live on a lonely planet. To break that cycle, I'm asking you to connect with the next person you meet or bump into. Practice being an encouraging and kind person. It doesn't have to be a grand gesture or long-winded conversation. Start small. Offer a smile, or a friendly greeting. Open the door for someone, or say thank you when someone does something small for you. Find two people today you can help out this way. Break that invisible barrier of our modern world. Break the social isolation and the loneliness and depression it brings. Make a friend; you might make someone's world just a little bit better. It's these small gestures that have the power to change the world as their ripple effect turns into something much bigger. We learn from each other what we need to experience in our own life to continue our process of personal growth and self-realization.

> *"Friends show their love in times of trouble, not in happiness."*
>
> *Euripides*

Anti-social media: is ignorance truly bliss?

The biggest problem I dealt with in building a business? There have been many, but the one I struggled with the most was not that people didn't buy what I was offering. It's not that everybody told me "I'm not interested". It's never been a lack of inspiration, time, or even money. It wasn't even the invoicing and bookkeeping part. Even though I'm not particularly good at numbers, all of that becomes relatively easy once you get the hang of it and establish a routine. The biggest struggle I dealt with was the fact nobody responds.

My litmus test was inviting "friends" on Facebook to events that I was organizing. I tried free events, paid events, online events, and "offline" events in real life. The same thing happened every time. The response rate to my invites was less than one percent. In marketing a one percent ratio is acceptable for cold leads. As a rule of thumb, out of one hundred people that never heard from you before, ten will be interested, and one will buy. But does the same rate apply to personal invitations, or even messages? Has ignoring become the new default response from people we're actually claim to be connected with?

The same goes for professional networking site LinkedIn. When my first book found a publishing home I got really excited and wrote individual, personalized emails to hundreds of connections. In my unbridled enthusiasm I imagined they all wanted at least one copy. I was certain if anyone of my connections had written a book I would certainly buy one, even if the writing were bad. It would just be cool to have a book on the shelf from someone you know. I think I might love books more than people. Those hundreds of messages resulted in two sales, and cramped fingers from all the typing. With the amount of money authors make on book royalties I could barely afford my usual quad shot black Americano for breakfast the next morning. Self-doubt kicked in. Did the lack of buy-in say something about people's perception of me, or about the quality of my writing?

Why is it you can call or text someone and they never reply back, but when you see them that phone is always in their hand? We're always connected but never connecting. What started as social media has gotten anti-social tendencies. Even "friends" who voluntarily connected with you have issues staying on top of their emails, messages, texts, and voicemails. They're too busy, and inundated with everything else that's going on in their life. Your message got lost in the mix with a thousand or so other notifications from their smart devices. We're overwhelmed with marketing messages from every possible angle. We receive thousands of impulses every day making demands of our already limited attention span. It makes it hard for a personal connection to stand out. It makes it even harder for a small business owner to stand out. The simultaneous shift to an artisan society further complicates the matter. For a while I considered going back to mail pigeons, but they don't seem to like Canadian winters either and flock to warmer places, smart as they are. I committed to figure out this modern day social issue on my own. Why was I able to sell boxes upon boxes of books at in-person speaking events and art markets, but has less success with connections in my first-degree network?

My initial conclusions were harsh. Usually I try to see the best in people, but for a small handful I was overly optimistic with my visions. There are people who will be there for you as long as you have something to offer they need. As soon as you no longer serve them a purpose, they are gone. While I'm grateful for those that did, I never expected all my friends and neighbors to line up at my events and buy my pictures, online courses, or books. Out of those, books turned out to be much easier to sell than fine art photography. Shelf space is easier to obtain than somebody's wall space, simply because they tend to have more of the one and less of the other.

> "Real knowledge is to know the extent of one's ignorance."
>
> *Confucius*

I no longer think it has to do with me, or the quality of my writing. The part I don't get is the ignoring of personal invitations, emails, and direct messages. Does inundation lead to ignorance? The social ignorance used to upset me. Isn't that the opposite of what social media tried to accomplish? In the end people will only treat you the way you allow them to. If you want to be treated differently, accept no less than what you deserve. And that's up to you, nobody else. Accountability is a beautiful thing.

The answer to my struggle is a new approach to networking. The problem is never "the rest of the world". Only a crazy man thinks they're sane themselves, whilst the rest of the world has lost their collective mind. Taking control and accountability means the problem solver is always me. By admitting I'm the crazy one, I can take responsibility for what I do next. By continuing to engage with the "mediocre club" I will continue to get the same results. That's not what I'm after. I'm looking to grow in life, learn and experience new things. I want to surround and associate myself with the people that share that mindset. Who's with me? Limit the time you spend with "friends" who are cynical and negative. The right network will create a supportive environment to help you grow and develop yourself more. Once you open yourself up for that opportunity, one by one those supportive people will start to appear. The focus shifts from old to new. The question is not if your network is ready, but are you?

Back to school

A while ago, I was asked to volunteer for a high school event. I loved the feeling of being back at high school, especially in North America with all the school buses parked out front. As a European immigrant school buses were only something I knew from the movies, and this day I I felt like I was a character in one of those movies. Being surrounded by so many students made me think back about my own high school years. I was pretty much the definition of a wallflower. I didn't have many friends and felt like the awkward kid in the class. Looking back there's so many things I wished I had done differently. Be less of a teachers pet for once, more of a badass. But I did no such thing. I was always focused on my homework, trying to impress everyone else: parents, teachers, and classmates.

The trend of trying to impress everyone carried on. Looking back years later, I wanted to tell my younger self so many things: "Lighten up. Live a little. You're awesome. Have fun. Don't worry so much about what others think. You'll be fine. I love you." A lot of modern day gurus make a lot of money repeating the previous sentence over and over again. They each have their own way of telling you exactly what you always wanted to hear. And while it makes us temporarily feel good, eventually the endorphin release wears off. When the expensive workshop or self-realization conference is over we're left with just ourselves. You still have to figure out what it all means in your own life. I used travel for that purpose: removing everything, and everyone familiar.

I ended up with just myself at the other end of the world; having to deal with all the same issues I started the journey with.

Despite of all the good intentions of modern day teachers and gurus, life doesn't quite work that way. You're on our own path, your own journey through life. You have to face your own demons, fight your own battles and learn from your own mistakes. In the online classes and programs I created, it's always been my focus to be very practical, without falling into to all too common trap of prescribing anyone what to do. I enjoy sharing my experiences to the benefit of others, but what you do with the models I developed based on those is ultimately up to you.

YOUR FAMILY

REDEFINING YOUR CLOSEST SUPPORT SYSTEM

Loving Your Family

When you're young, you believe everything. Your father is the strongest man. Santa Claus is real. But there will be a day when you'll realize none of it is true. That faint rumour in the back of your mind turns out the be the reality instead. The idea that a big fat man flies halfway across the world to deliver presents is insane.

So, we grow up, growing a little more unhappy every year. The only moments when you feel like you used to, is when you fall in love. The moments where you love someone, for real. In those moments anything that's unhappy disappears for a while - as if it faded into the background. Love is everything - and that's what we're supposed to believe in and hold on to.

So what if we all decide to agree that Santa Claus is for real? We'd still have to buy the presents ourselves - but it's the idea that counts. The idea, or belief, that we will prevail in the end, that love will prevail in the end. Because love is like Santa Claus - you have to believe it, or it's never going to work.

Love Is All

We're all from different countries

When I played outside as a kid and I considered the amount of noise we produced as a legitimate indicator of the amount of fun we were having, my mom would strongly object to those assumptions. A firm "be quiet" would set us back on the right track. Her approach to parenting seems to have grown out of date, unfortunately. When I'm working in my home office at the front of the house I sometimes wonder if the neighborhood children, playing in the back of their house, are physically ok. The amount of yelling and screaming might indicate, from a layman's perspective, they are not. It seems the more fun they're having the louder it gets. Hal Edward Runkel wrote a wonderful book on Scream Free Parenting, which I'm considering buying in bulk for the young parents on my street. It might help them keep their offspring in line.

The idea of a modern family is typically made up of three ingredients: nice home, enough money, and good relationships. Even if problems arise, the family stays together to face life as a "team". Family is where we hope to find historical roots, a sense of comfort and security, acceptance, love, and mutual support. Bestselling author and humorist Erma Louise Bombeck described a typical suburban family as a "strange little band of characters trudging through life sharing diseases and toothpaste, coveting one another's desserts, hiding shampoo, borrowing money, locking each other out of our rooms, inflicting pain and kissing to heal it in the same instant, loving, laughing, defending, and trying to figure out the common thread that bound us all together."

Not all families turn out to be happy. Not everyone has a family waiting at home. For those that do, eight out of ten families are considered dysfunctional at some level. Most families experience heartbreak and break-ups, leaving both the married couple and their dependent children in a state of depression. In addition to issues of separation and divorce, common family struggles include the death of a loved one, financial difficulties, and parent-child conflicts. Dealing with a problem inside a family can be one of the most difficult experiences in life. While the idea of a family is perceived to be a support system, reality is often far from it. We're raised and conditioned with that ideal family picture. When the family structure crumbles under the pressure of reality, along with it we lose the ideas of unconditional love, safety, and all the things in between.

Creating distance to get closer

Angela grew up in a family where she was the caretaker. She naturally grew into that role, and everybody else in the family accepted that model. Angela was not a happy child. As the older sibling of two, Angela was the caring, empathetic and compassionate individual the family needed. It was only natural for her to always protect her younger sister from their father's physical and emotional abuse. Eventually, even her mother learned to turn to Angela for help and protection. Because everyone learned to rely on her, when things didn't turn out the way they wanted, Angela was the one they blamed. Angela became an invisible child. Because of her sensitivity to other people's feelings and needs, her own feelings and needs went unnoticed. Everyone in her family wanted to take from her, but no one wanted to give to her.

As an adult, Angela did a lot of inner healing work. I met Angela at a corporate retreat we both attended. She discovered that she had been conditioned to ignore her own feelings and needs. She structured her entire life around the idea of always putting others before herself. There's nothing wrong with

> *"Do we need distance to get close?"*
> Sarah Jessica Parker

selfless care for others, but on it's own the idea is overrated. You can only give away what you have enough of. If you're not taken care of yourself you'll eventually end up running on emotional fumes, literally. For the first time, Angela learned to take loving care of her own wants and needs. She learned to let go of taking responsibility for everyone else. Her family became furious with her, wondering why she became so selfish. They felt abandoned. The blame that Angela already had experienced from her family in the past intensified. She tried to explain herself, but nothing she said had any impact on her family's behavior toward her. They refused to support her. They just wanted things to go back to the way they had always been.

Angela finally decided that, although she loved her family, she needed to distance herself from them. To allow her family to continue to treat her badly limited her own growth and development. She had to disengage with the ways the family had always operated. While she couldn't change how her family treated her, she could control her response to that behavior. Angela broke almost all communication with her family for three years. Initially it didn't benefit the relationship. Angela's distance caused her parents and sister to blame her even more. During the few times that Angela communicated with her mother, the hostility was intense. "What is the matter with you? Have you gone nuts? How can you abandon your family? You are being so selfish! Don't you care about us?" Angela knew that it was useless to try to defend herself against these allegations. Her mother didn't really want to engage in a conversation about the answers to these questions, but instead continued exercising her manipulating control. It took three years before anyone in her family started to treat Angela with any sense of respect. It took a complete breakdown

> *"Happiness is having a large, loving, caring, close-knit family in another city."*
>
> George Burns

of communication over an extended period of time before the family accepted that they could no longer treat her badly if they wanted a relationship with her. Today, Angela has a much better relationship with her family.

A detour to Paris and Barcelona

There are a lot of similarities between Angela's story and mine. I haven't seen my family for almost three years now. I blame the Atlantic Ocean, but the responsibility for choosing to live on the other side of it is entirely my own. Living this far away is not always easy, especially when Christmas and birthdays come around. The feeling of missing people is equally upsetting even if I'm the one who decided to follow a dream and move to the other side of the planet.

While it was never my intention to completely lose touch with my family, they did lose their front-row seats in the theater of my life. As a dear friend so delicately worded it, for a while it was necessary for them to be outside the theater, to be later re-admitted in standing room only. The question of missing or even losing touch with family has to come up when moving halfway across the globe. No matter how easy it is to stay in touch through the Internet, the physical separation does irreversibly change the relationship. Through cultural conditioning, most people have been taught that it is wrong to disengage from family. No matter how bad your father treated you, we always say, "it's still your dad". It's engrained in our brain to keep the family unit intact at all costs. We'd rather sacrifice our own dreams for the sake of the family, than being perceived as selfish. When I first announced the intent of wanting to move to the other side of the Atlantic, I've been called selfish. Many other allegations were added to that list as the plans progressed and the departure day neared. Mentioning Canada at family events became synonymous with profanity, and was subsequently banned from the conversation. The problem with these deep-rooted limiting beliefs about family is that it gives a person who is being blamed and disrespected by their family, no way out. It's a behavior that you'll get used to over many years of mental conditioning. We would never allow a stranger to treat us the way our family treats us. Yet when it comes to family we are afraid to speak up for ourselves. Because "it's still family", you tell yourself. No matter how emotionally abusive the family relationship may be, the guilt trip continues.

After I moved to Canada, it was my goal to go back every three years to visit my family. Those three-year periods go by quickly, and after six years in Canada I booked my second trip to the homeland. With a credit card high score in my pocket for non-refundable transatlantic airfare I phoned my family to share the happy news of my planned visit. That turned out to be a bad idea. They had been planning to book a vacation at the same time, and although nothing had been booked yet the intent was, for various reasons, to proceed with that plan. I instantly regretted booking my trip, and for a few days I considered calling the whole thing off despite the non-changeable airfare. Ultimately I wanted to fly home not just to see my family, but also to spend a few days in the country I grew up in. Simple familiarities can be boring, but then again comforting if you remove yourself long enough. I ended up spending less time with my family than I had originally imagined. It was for the better. Sometimes the most loving act, both for you and for others, is to disengage from a troubled relationship. It is not right to allow yourself to be treated disrespectfully. Allowing anyone to treat you with disrespect makes you an enabler

> *"Paris is always a good idea"*
>
> Audrey Hepburn

of that interaction for as long as you allow it to continue to happen. It might mean you have to make a difficult decision. This black sheep of the family definitely had to adjust his expectations. I ended up going to Paris for a few days instead, which still happens to be one of my favorite cities in the world. On my next trip home I might go to Barcelona, a place I've always wanted to visit. Maybe I'll even make a Mediterranean cruise, something I never even thought I'd be interested in doing.

Over the years, my trips home have taught me that I value family more than I originally thought. I also learned the family experience I craved could not be had with my family, at least not at that time. On the almost nine hour flight back to Canada, I appreciated the Atlantic Ocean for providing some much needed distance and peace of mind. I asked myself why I always wanted to fix the relationship I had with my family, and for who? What is it that I truly wanted out of that relationship? On that plane ride home, I committed to being happy on my own first of all. Years later, my dear friend Jack Canfield gave me this advice: "If your family's negativity is slowly poisoning you, have an honest talk with them and tell them how their negative words and actions affect you. If they don't listen to you or honor how you feel, stop spending time with them. You have the power, and the right, to remove people from your life if they constantly attack your sense of self worth and are preventing you from becoming the best possible person you can be." Guilt trips aside, it really can be that simple. One of my ultimate relationship goals, in general, is to only want good for the other person. I still live by that rule. Wanting good for someone else does not mean it should be bad for me. At some point you'll have to allow yourself to admit that your line in the sand was crossed, and take a few steps back.

Making a move across the Atlantic Ocean changes the relationship with everything in your life, including yourself. The changing relationship with others is more or less obvious: adding an ocean in between a friendship or family has to change the dynamic. The one thing you can't leave behind is yourself. In a new environment where literally everything is different, you're left with just you, having to face all the harsh realities about yourself that you were able to tuck away in between your comfortable, familiar surroundings. Family is still my basic social unit, but the definition changed. Family represents people living together by ties of marriage, blood, or otherwise representing a single household. Those you consider family are not just the people who are blood related, but more often the loved ones who connect to you in friendship, love and respect. Blood might make you related; it does not make you family. Loving someone, standing by their side and supporting them are what really make you family.

Fast-forward eighteen years

My story about being the black sheep of the family doesn't include my father. Him and my mom got divorced, twice, from each other. As a teenager, I took that matter seriously. And wanting to support my mom, I got too involved in the divorce process and saw things I shouldn't have at that age. Looking back it all made more sense, at the time I was just trying to help. The second time around, my dad had already left, or quite possibly been forced to leave. The rest I heard from him was through his lawyer, and from my mom. Years later you have to ask the question how colored the picture was that was painted of him. It sure didn't leave me with warm and fuzzy feelings, and I lived my adolescence and many years beyond that without any contact.

Despite my resistance to social media, as an author I've maintained a presence on all major social media networks. I've always encouraged people to connect with me there and enjoy staying in touch with my community. For the work I do, it's more or less mandatory to maintain a partially public persona. And sure enough, eighteen years later, literally weeks before this book went to press there was a message, but not from my father. A woman, judging by the photographs his new partner, had commented on one of my post about not seeing my family for years. The article itself was unrelated to her question, but the title "The Black Sheep" must have spurred some interest and made them think of me. The message, loosely translated, commented briefly on how I hadn't seen my family for years, but my dad for much longer. "Why?", she asked.

With an eight-hour time difference between Canada and Europe unexpected messages from the old homeland always seem to show up when I'm having my morning coffee, so admitted I was a bit shaken up. Eighteen years is a long time. I've moved past the accusing statement "it's still family", or in this case, "it's still your dad" a long time ago. But here it was again, yet in slightly different form. Written on a public Facebook wall by a woman I had never heard of. The question she was asking was probably more a rhetorical statement, expressing her own confusion about our family's troubled past. I wholeheartedly agree. The existence of those questions itself explains at least part of the "why", but I wasn't sure I was about to dive into that with someone I had never met or spoken to before. Because of her undoubtedly good intentions, I wrote back a brief friendly response but left it at that.

The thing with questions is that the mind will force you to find an answer. If I ask any random stranger how much money they make, they're unlikely to answer, even though their mind will immediately bring the requested information to the forefront of their brain. Reading this, you probably think about that number right now. For me, the unexpected question prompted more questions. Indeed, "why?" Taking a passive stance like I did means you might be waiting for a long time. For anything you truly want, I don't recommend you go about it as passive as I did. But did I truly want a close relationship with my family? I think reality has moved passed that point, even though we're still family, and there is always room for new and improved relationships. You never know what might happen tomorrow morning over coffee.

All you need is love

After the Second World War, many people wanted to start a new life on the other side of the ocean. The war had destroyed much of the European economy, and instead of waiting years for it to recover people opted to move abroad. Canada, Australia and the United States were among some of the most popular destinations for Dutch emigrants. For them, their transatlantic move was literally a one-way ticket by boat. Making the move would take everything they had left, and if it didn't work out there was no way back. Staying in touch with family and friends left behind was difficult. Until later in the fifties, there was no transatlantic telephone service, so the only option was to write and wait for the mail to arrive. It would take weeks if not months to hear back, as long as the mail didn't get lost somewhere along the way.

Staying in touch with family abroad has become a lot easier. Today, I can even watch some Dutch television shows on my Canadian flat screen. Through the various media players available these days, it's become a relatively easy process, despite some of the providers making it unnecessarily difficult by adding location-based filters to their online video streams. One of the shows I enjoy watching is a program called All You Need Is Love. In particular their Christmas Eve episode has became a tradition for me every holiday season abroad. The host, Robert ten Brink, has made it his life work to reunite families and loved ones that have been separated by distance for a long time. Many of the stories are in one way or another influenced by families who were separated by the post war mass emigration. Absence makes the hard grow fonder. Distance is hard but can result in something good. In any case, it makes for many years of great television.

What strikes me most every time when watching Robert reunite families on All You Need Is Love, is that missing someone isn't a bad thing. It's a good thing, a beautiful thing even. We experience "missing" someone often as a negative emotion, but it doesn't have to be. While physical separation changes the relationship, it doesn't mean the change can't be for the better. Interactions might be less frequent, but are often more intense in the short amounts of time you do get to spend together.

When you're extremely close to your family you probably won't do what I did. You won't move to the other side of the Atlantic Ocean to chase some version of the American Dream in Canada. While I love my family, the pull of adventure was stronger for me than family bonds. My move ultimately forced the relationships I had with my family and friends to be redefined. Some improved for the better, some became worse, and others disappeared completely. There are different people that play different roles in every stage of life. The cast of your life's theater is ever changing.

> *"Sometimes, only one person is missing, and the whole world seems depopulated."*
>
> Alphonse de Lamartine

In a way, I love my family more now that I'm on the other side of the Atlantic Ocean. It changed the dynamic of the relationship, which doesn't have to be a bad thing. My family, on the other hand, never approved of my move abroad. If you fear the unknown, that's where I live. With every major setback I faced in building a life in Canada, it was expected I would return home. I never did. Even though I might eventually move on to another place, I'm not planning on ever returning home permanently. Aside from the complicated paperwork, immigration is an irreversible process that "de-roots" you. The wanderlust is part of my genetic structure. From time to time it makes me restless, but hardly ever homesick.

Dealing with death while abroad

I knew it was coming at some point. Ever after packing my bags, even in preparation before departure, I knew that eventually I too would get that dreaded phone call from the old homeland informing me a family member had passed away, or was about to. After all, one of the few certainties in life is that none of us will make it out alive. When that happens, you'd have to ask whether jumping on a transatlantic flight with virtually no notice is the right investment of time and money. To prepare for this unavoidable event, I created a list of names prior to my departure, detailing exactly what to do when that moment would arrive. Who would I fly back for, and under what circumstance? With all the added emotion and possible pressure from people to fly back instantly it's better to allow yourself the luxury of being prepared as best as you can be. Because when, not if, it happens, there will be plenty of unforeseen things to deal with anyway, even if it was just the emotional side of things.

For me, the unavoidable phone call I had tried to prepare myself for came in the form of an unexpected text message. Despite all the preparation, the unforeseen form in which the message arrived caught me off guard. I read it while having my usual early morning coffee. After being ill for some time, my grandfather (opa, in Dutch) had passed away. Nothing could have prepared me for the cold reality on that winter morning. With the funeral being planned for literally days later, it was impossible to even attempt to fly back and attend it. When something urgent or unexpected happens, you're not going to make it back fast enough if you live this far away. After being in Canada for ten years, I've missed weddings, funerals, divorces, birthday parties and many other events. Some I was invited to, others I didn't even know about.

The one unexpected trip home I did make was to see my "other" grandpa at least once more. He wasn't grandma's first husband, so technically speaking not even my biological grandpa. To me he's always been the most family imaginable. As a child I had developed an irrational homesickness, which abruptly ended the sleepovers I always enjoyed prior. Through endless patience he helped me overcome this fear, eventually making me feel comfortable to sleep in other beds but my own again. He might have put in the foundation for my future travels all around the world, helping me feel at home everywhere I go. When I heard opa was diagnosed with various types of cancer, I called him a few days later. When we spoke on the phone, it seemed he hadn't changed much. Despite his life threatening condition, he was doing well given the circumstances, still being lively and energetic. I called my travel agent and she got me on a flight to Amsterdam. The purpose of that impromptu trip wasn't to say goodbye, but to have a cup of coffee with a man that had meant so much to me. I never wanted the last memory to be anyone's deathbed, but the stories we shared over coffee, and Dutch treats. It's about those last memories we carry with us. Make them count.

> *"No matter how prepared you think you are for the death of a loved one, it still comes as a shock, and it still hurts very deeply."*
>
> Billy Graham

Weddings and funerals

People tend to be at their best-worst behavior at weddings and funerals. These two major life events bring out the best in us. We dress up nicely, and feel more or less obligated to attend the event, even for any far removed half-relatives we barely know or spend time with on a regular basis. Under those nice layers of designer fabrics we come armed with a lot of ideas, thoughts and expectations as to how the day will, or should, unfold. Expectations of how it should be in case of weddings, and usually how it should have been in case of funerals. "It" either refers to the life of the deceased, or newly wed couple. What a way to celebrate the start, or end, of (married) life.

As a professional photographer, I used to attend the occasional wedding or two. Most wedding invites I get from friends come with a little handwritten "PS": "you'll bring your camera, right?" I used to, but not anymore. For a few weddings and family events I even got paid. The money I made funded a large portion of my initial fine art activities. Gear doesn't come cheap, and while unpaid exposure at small events is nice, it doesn't pay my bills. Later on, I gave up on the photo shoot business completely. I decided to focus my creative career exclusively on the fine art space. I love photography as a medium, but for me the medium was about sharing stories, and the ability to give back some of my travel memories to the world.

Here's my unsolicited advice to any couple that wants to get married. First of all, it's your special day, so make it special for you.

Your family and friends are provided free food and free drinks so they shouldn't be too demanding in regards to the agenda for the big day. Unless you're having a cash bar, in which case don't bother inviting me. Cash bars at weddings were my second-biggest topic of culture shock in Canada, in particular the one where I was charged seven dollars for a glass of home-made wine that tasted like lemonade. Needless to say the party was short-lived. So let me rephrase my first piece of wedding advice. Make it your special day, as long as there's no cash bar. Secondly, don't cheap out on your photographer. You don't hire one for just any ordinary day so make sure to hire the one that's right for you. I've been asked to reshoot weddings one too many times for couples that thought they could save a few dollars on their photographer for the day. To be clear, I don't do that anymore, either.

The same advice applies to funerals, in a way. Do it your way, life that is. Looking back, most regrets are for things we didn't end up doing. The poem "Moments", which I included in my first book, and have since read at many of my public speaking events, describes it best. The poem is often incorrectly attributed to Argentine writer Jorge Luis Borges, but the original author remains unknown.

> *If I could live again my life,*
> *In the next – I'll try,*
> *– to make more mistakes,*
> *I won't try to be so perfect,*
> *I'll be more relaxed,*
> *I'll be more full – than I am now,*
> *In fact, I'll take fewer things seriously,*
> *I'll be less hygienic,*

I'll take more risks,
I'll take more trips,
I'll watch more sunsets,
I'll climb more mountains,
I'll swim more rivers,
I'll go to more places – I've never been,
I'll eat more ice creams and less (lime) beans,
I'll have more real problems – and less imaginary ones,
I was one of those people who live
prudent and prolific lives –
each minute of his life,
Of course that I had moments of joy – but,
if I could go back I'll try to have only good moments,
If you don't know – that's what life is made of,
Don't lose the now!
I was one of those who never goes anywhere
without a thermometer,
without a hot-water bottle,
and without an umbrella and without a parachute,
If I could live again – I will travel light,
If I could live again – I'll try to work bare feet
at the beginning of spring till the end of autumn,
I'll ride more carts,
I'll watch more sunrises and play with more children,
If I have the life to live – but now I am 85,
– and I know that I am dying …

The importance of family

Family to me is more important than I was willing to admit. My resistance to family was founded in what I was experiencing in reality. The fact that the relationship wasn't fulfilling increased the sense of importance I felt for my unfulfilled idea of having a family experience in my life. I attempted to do more to please everybody else. I tried everything under the sun to make them happy. At the same time, I also tried building my own life in Canada. That transatlantic move didn't help them much at all, but despite the setbacks eventually the move did help me. Even when you're the one leaving, you'll still have feelings of loss and missing people. Missing people is a good thing, as it will make the heart grow fonder. The ocean gives a new sense of perspective. The physical separation initially created a newfound appreciation. I still took the blame for my move. After all, I was the one who left everything behind. "Naturally" that decision and its consequences were entirely my responsibility.

I got so busy trying to accommodate everybody else's feelings that I forgot about my own. The thing about travel, and particularly moving to a foreign country, is that all those built up issues you never dealt with will come to the forefront in full force. This is why travel is a catalyst for personal growth, if you're prepared for it and willing to take advantage of the opportunity created by unfamiliar territory.

It doesn't mean I don't miss people from my past, but there's a reason they didn't make it into my future. If people are in your past they're there for a reason. It doesn't mean they need to be in your future. They can be, but it doesn't have to be that way. Regardless of whether or not these people are your family, friends, or your partner. Maybe you're even married to them. It doesn't matter. If people don't treat you well, they might be in your life today, but nobody has guaranteed reserved seating for the future. For some people standing room is a better place, or they might need to be out of the theater completely for a while. All the value we've been trained to assign to about family, parents, brothers, sisters, husbands and wives is mental conditioning at it's finest. Conditioning can be toxic.

Now don't get me wrong. People are important. Family, in the end, is more important to me than I've been willing to admit for a long time. The physical separation underlines that importance. I'm not advocating a life in solitary confinement. But stop placing perceived ideas about others and their relationship to you above your own health and well being. It's ok to miss someone.

SOMEONE SPECIAL

FIGHTING FOR WHO MATTERS MOST

Loving Someone Special

People who get married are not to be trusted. You know why? Because if you were legitimately happy, honestly you wouldn't feel the need to make a big show out of it. You wouldn't have to broadcast it. They do it because they're insecure and because they think that getting married is what they're supposed to be doing now. And so they're lying to themselves and they're lying to others.

He's Just Not That Into You

The stage gates of life

Have you ever run into an old friend, that you didn't see for at least a few years? What excuses did either of you came up with for having lost touch? Thanks to all the traveling I do, I'm happy to have friends all over the world. Most of those friends I probably won't see more than a few times in this life, but we make a mutual effort to stay in touch. I ran into someone the other day that lives relatively close to me. I hadn't seen him since his wedding day, which was over a year ago. The excuse he shared with me? "I'm so busy parenting."

I don't have any kids, except my beloved fur babies. Given my lifestyle that's probably for the better. Regardless, the encounter with my old friend suggested there are certain stage gates in the life of a relationship. To name a few examples: getting married, becoming parents, and getting divorced. The divorce might seem optional, but statistically speaking it isn't. As people cross over each bridge in life and move over to the next phase, they seem to suffer from the temporary illusion that they have finally arrived. You're one level up in the game of life, having left behind the unlucky ones who haven't made it there quite yet.

> *"I never lost a friend I wanted to keep."*
> Walter Winchell

As long as there's another bridge to cross, you've never truly made it. If you just got married you obviously haven't made it to the divorce level yet. It might not even be in sight, let alone on your mind. You just got married. After completing that interpersonal merger you're within your self-entitled right of feeling better than the rest of your friends. You're up one level. Since you have arrived, connections with those who haven't made it there yet, feel less natural, less necessary even. The ideal of monogamy appears to be based on exclusion, and it starts right there. As the couple grows together and builds a life, more and more people are excluded from that relationship the further it progresses.

Lies, damn lies, and statistics

Relationships aren't easy, they say. Love isn't easy, but that's why they call it love. The concept of human interrelations on a romantic level isn't easy, or is it? The statistics are daunting. Divorce and separation rates are at an all-time high. The idea we stay with the same partner until death do us part is, for better or worse, no longer a reality in today's world. And it doesn't get better. Arguing the first marriage failed because of young age is too simplistic, as the odds get worse over time. You'd think that in a second or third marriage the numbers improve. You'd expect that maybe we'd know what we'd be looking for the next time around. The opposite is true. Divorce rates climb even higher for second and third marriages. It's like everyone has collectively adopted one of my Living by Experience concepts: making the same mistakes again, just faster. Most relationships end in divorce or separation, but this destiny is not unavoidable. You have to give individual people a shot at beating the odds. Why else do we flock en masse to Las Vegas? Call me a romantic, but true unselfish love does happen, maybe just not very often.

The key is in the premise, or the foundation, of the relationship. Unless you are totally happy on your own, and meet someone who is also totally happy to be on their own, you will experience conflicts in your relationship. The combination of being totally happy on your own, and finding someone else who is too, seems like winning the dating lottery. Not impossible, but once again the odds aren't in your favor. Most of us are attempting to find another person to fill in the blanks in our own life. Both partners are trying to get the other partner to be the way they want them to be. Have you ever heard anyone say, "opposites attract", or call someone their "better half"? We're looking for the qualities of another person to make us whole.

True happiness cannot be found on the outside. Happiness starts with you, as an inner state. Happiness is being loved for who you are, without any external expectations or conditions. One of my most favorite quotes from the movie Moulin Rouge is when Ewan McGregor, as his character Christian says, "The greatest thing you'll ever learn is just to love and be loved in return." There's immediacy to that statement. Love, and being loved, is not something far away. Love is now. It's the present. Christian describes that mental state of being in the now. Many people only see love, just like travel and happiness, somewhere in their future, as if it was an ultimate goal. It's not a reality today, but the goal is definitely on the horizon. Happiness, love and even travel have very little to do with the future, but everything with the here and now. Freedom is about this moment. The problem with the horizon is that it's a non-existent, imaginary line. We are looking for things to be the way we want them to be before we can be happy. If you live by that model, you'll never get where you want to be, as freedom will always remain on the horizon. You can never reach the imaginary finish line. Unless you still believe the world is flat, you'll never get there. I've flown all around this planet, and take my word for it if you must; planet earth is not flat. The majority of couples live in conflict today because they do believe the world if flat: they're still trying to get to the horizon.

In another favorite movie of mine, One Week, Ben Tyler, played by Joshua Jackson, has been diagnosed with cancer. Foregoing his required treatment, he instead decides to take a motorcycle trip from Toronto across Canada to Vancouver Island. Along the way, he meets several people that help him reevaluate his relationship with his fiancée, his job, and his dream of becoming a writer. In dealing with cancer, Ben's chance of survival is limited, but, as his doctor says, when you're dealing with individuals, you have to throw the numbers out. In the end of the movie, the same is said about relationships. It doesn't matter how high or low divorce rates or cancer survival rates are, when you're dealing with individuals you have to consider the chance that those individuals beat the odds and make it through.

Judging by the daunting numbers and other bad press about marriage and relationships, it seems virtually impossible to stay free and happy in one or the other. Yet married life is the common ideal in most areas of the world, in particular North America. We're committed to holding on to an ancient relationship model, even if it no longer seems to serve us well. We all cherish the idea of being in a relationship, and eventually marriage. The online dating industry generates billions in revenue each year, because we want to be in a life that's safe, secure and predictable. What it really means is that you want to be free, and your partner to be the way you want him or her to be. We want predictable, whilst minimizing risk. The odds, again, are not in your favor. It's time to look for an alternative strategy, an upgraded view. Sometimes love is not knowing the whole story, or going after a different story altogether.

Visiting the city of love and light

Visiting the city of light and love, Paris, is a dream of many. But on one of my trips there, things went horribly wrong. After an enjoyable high-speed train ride from Amsterdam, and looking forward to a few relaxing days in Paris, I arrived at the wrong hotel. There turned out to be two hotels, with exactly the same name. Thanks, Expedia. The first one, where we showed up, met all the expectations. The hotel was exactly like the reviews and online pictures had suggested. However the receptionist had no record of our reservation. The other one, the one we apparently had booked, did not meet the expectations, by any means. The place was a dump, to put it nicely. Registration didn't even involve checking identification, which is a safety standard common in the travel industry worldwide. I could only guess what this "hotel" was mostly used for. They probably had an unadvertised hourly rate.

The room was nothing short of the looks and smells of a brothel. I felt unsafe, and left within five minutes after checking in. I didn't even care about losing the pre-paid rate. My health, safety and wellbeing were more important. The first night was nothing like the Parisian love and light I had grown accustomed to during my many visits in the years prior. I ended up lost and confused, like in a bad love affair. Travel will do that to you from time to time. I was tired and had no idea where to go next. All hotels in the area seemed fully booked, and those with a room or two available charged upwards of a thousand euros a night. On top of that, the exchange rate against my Canadian bank accounts did not work out in my favor. Everything was "complete", which is French for fully booked.

I found myself homeless on the streets of Paris. It was early in the evening, and the sun was starting to set. I was tired, angry, and frustrated. We frantically roamed the streets for several hours, looking for a place to sleep. I was even questioned by the local police, the Gendarmerie, who seemed concerned but unable to do anything. We made it to the Champs Elysees, one of my favorite streets to come to for an evening stroll or late night drink. None of that was on the agenda today, but luckily we did find a room for upwards of three hundred euros a night. "Welcome to Paris", the receptionist said after swiping my credit card. When I figured out the exchange rate, I suddenly understood people who say they love Paris, but hate the French. I physically collapsed when I made it up to the room. Excited to finally have a place to rest my jet-lagged mind, my body decided it had enough of travel. Ending up nearly homeless on the streets of Paris was not what travel was supposed to be about. I vouched to never book on the same travel site again, and only use verified, curated hotel booking sites going forward.

The evening ended with a nice dinner, followed by a restless night, despite the expensive room. I've had some interesting experiences before exploring the world, but this was the first time where I needed to call in for support and secure alternate travel arrangements from my travel agent back home. I never imagined Paris could be scary place, but when the sun starts to set and you have no place to sleep, things can change quickly. In my travel book in this Freedom Project series I share all my insights about picking a place to stay while traveling. In a nutshell, it's about location, location, location. On this trip to Paris I completely failed. Did I not follow my own steps and guidelines while booking the hotel? Quite the contrary is true. I practice what I preach, and followed all of them. I researched reviews, and used a well-known, major booking site to make the reservation. After this trip, I switched from using travel agents to a travel designer. What ended me in this mess was the simple overabundance of hotels. There were too many options to pick from, and with confusing similar names it didn't take long to get into trouble.

> *"An artist has no home in Europe except in Paris."*
> — Friedrich Nietzsche

This trip shook me up. It took a stab at an inherent feeling of safety and being at home anywhere in the world, no matter how uncomfortable or unfamiliar the circumstances. I went home with a difficult question on my mind that demanded to be answered. That almost-failed trip to the city of light and love reduced me to the bare essence: did I want to be in a relationship, period. I instinctively knew I did, but not in the traditional sense of the word. That created a new question. What defines a non-traditional relationship? Feeling unconditionally loved and supported were two of the main ingredients of the relationship I was after this time around. I knew I wanted to write our own rules, even though I wasn't sure by any means what those rules would be in order to make me happy.

The battle between love and your ego

Happiness and freedom are on most people's bucket list. Do you long for love as well? Most of us do. We do not like our current reality. We don't like how we feel inside most of the time. The roots of our unhappiness may lie in an unpleasant childhood, or other traumatizing experiences from the more recent past. We're looking to make up for those things in a relationship. A relationship can hide those emotions and negative experiences. Being in love can be a good hiding place. The intimate touch of another human being is the most powerful antidote for the all-too-human experience of loneliness. Feeling loved and cared for may be the most compelling and pleasurable experience there is. Yet in reality we spend so much of our time and energy avoiding intimacy by building walls, defending ourselves, being angry, critical, closed off and judgmental. We're blocking the experience that we most deeply want. We are wired to reinforce our limited ego-based identity, our sense of who we truly are. Much like I did when I moved across the planet, you'll always bring yourself with you into any relationship you enter. If you can pick your own family, you definitely have to pick your own partner, from a position of freedom. For most that means a different partner for certain stages of our life, whether short or long term.

Our ego-based identity plays a very important role finding and selecting a partner, but in itself the ego does not have the power to love. Ego is a your sense of self-esteem or self-importance. It's all about the self. It can however experience need, and need is often easy to mistake for love. The ego can definitely love the experience of how another person makes it feel. But external experiences that someone else does to you aren't true love. True love and intimacy doesn't come from the ego. In order to experience the power of true love you have to get in touch with a different part of yourself, a part that lives beyond your ego.

This process is easier when you understand the true nature of your ego-based identity. Ego doesn't exist. Sorry, Freud. Although the ego functions as if it's the most real thing about you, your "identity" is only a perspective. It's the way your inner critic views you. The idea of the ego is kept alive by the little voice in your head that tells you stories about life, others and yourself. Your ego is all talk, more specifically, self-talk. Ego is a negative, unpleasant monologue. The ego tries to define who you are and who you aren't, generally by comparing and relating to the people, ideas, and objects in your environment. The ego is a mind trick. Ego is an idea our mind has invented to keep our negative self-talk alive and justify it.

The contradiction of love and freedom

Have you ever seen the popular "game over" stag T-shirt? It's available in many different designs and versions now, but originally the shirt started with the silhouette of a groom wearing a ball and chain beside his new bride. "Game over", the caption said. Love and freedom are opposing ideas, which don't seem to go hand-in-hand, unlike the newly married couple. In some variations of the shirt the groom would be even depicted with a frowning face, while the bride is smiling. Is this how we're collectively thinking about marriage?

When a couple first meets, at least one person, but with any luck both people, are attracted to the other party. The other person stands out from the crowd. Thinking back to your first date, you might see you were fun, outgoing, and exceptionally alive. Then as the relationship progressed, conditions and limitations were added to the rules of engagement. If the couple stays together, those rules are not to be broken. One of the main rules is not to be attracted to anyone else ever again. The rules of engagement attempt to control the outgoing, bubbly character of the first date; eventually limiting it's every move. For the sake of the relationship, one or both partners have disconnected from their original feeling of freedom. They become ordinary, normal, and ultimately boring. Over time, the relationship kills those very things that created the initial attraction. The spark literally fades away. It doesn't matter how in love you initially felt or still may feel. If the other partner in the relationship has conditions for that relationship, sooner or later there's going to be a problem.

In the human mind, freedom is relative to your current situation. Our dualistic mind thinks the grass is always greener on the other side of the fence. In my Happiness book I explored the common misperception that freedom in a career comes from being an entrepreneur instead of an employee. We all think we want to work for ourselves instead of working for someone else. I've been depressed, stressed and burned out on both sides of that often-debated fence. Many people climb to the top of their career ladder, only to find out the ladder was against the wrong wall by the time they made it nearly all the way there.

Most humans think they are superior to animals. As Paul Lowe says, animal lives consist of the three F's: feeding, fighting, and reproduction. Sounds familiar? In a relationship, people think they're free. We make ourselves believe we're doing well, as long as the other person doesn't talk about a certain person in their past or family, or doesn't exhibit a certain behavior we don't like. The relationship is like an invisible dog fence. I often see those fences advertised around the rural farmhouses and acreages of Southern Alberta. At one point I considered buying one of those fences. My German Shepherd dog used to live on a large farm. She's a roamer. She doesn't take off and to run for the hills, but she does like to wander around and make new friends. The idea behind the electric fence is simple. The minute a dog gets to the perimeter, it gets a small electric shock. Sounds evil, but the companies that make these things claim they're pet-friendly. Learning where the boundaries are, the dog learns and remembers how far it can go. As pet owners, the electric fence allows us to feel safe and secure without having to watch the animal's every move. For some, installing a similar invisible fence into their relationship might sound like a wonderful idea. Maybe you have one operational already. Is it going to work long term? My dog is too smart for her own good, and I'm sure eventually she would have figured out the weak spots that exist in most boundaries. Systems aren't flawless. She'd take a good running start, take off toward the perimeter, take the shock for granted and bust right through to freedom. Isn't the intelligence of dogs amazing?

The love a dog feels for their owner is unconditional. It doesn't matter how upset I get with my canine companion over something she's destroyed in my house or yard. She'll still want to go for a walk or have a belly rub within minutes after I got mad. Dogs don't hold on to grudges. Whether or not that's animal intelligence or lack thereof goes beyond the scope of this book, but for the sake of this argument let's give them the benefit of the doubt. My dog didn't want to escape. She just enjoyed roaming around the large property and making friends with neighboring farm animals. One day I was extremely worried when she had been gone for several hours. When I finally found her in the midst of a group of cows, she couldn't be happier to see me. She didn't need an electric fence to keep her coming back to me.

> *"The secret to happiness is freedom... And the secret to freedom is courage."*
>
> Thucydides

The true concept of freedom is an absolute. Freedom doesn't have any conditions. True freedom is without compromise, and has no fear. Freedom means you don't make concessions, and don't settle. How free do you feel today? Is there any compromise, or electric fence in your life? If so, take care of it, or stop complaining about it. You are as free as you allow yourself to be. Ultimately, it's a yes or no question. No need for an electric fence, or other arbitrary provisions.

People, myself included, are afraid of losing their partner. They might die, or go away. Eventually everybody dies, or goes away. "This too shall pass" is a saying I've relied on to get through difficult times in my life. Originally a Persian saying, it reflects on the temporary nature of our life in general: good and bad. Maybe you woke up feeling depressed today. For a long time I did, and told myself, "I know things will happen today, become clearer and help with the next steps. By end of this day I will feel better." Although it took a little longer, eventually that too did pass. Everything is fleeting, the good things will pass, and the bad things will pass. The key is to accept life as it is, in this moment. Freedom is maximized when you're living right here, in the now. Adjust and adapt yourself to situations as much as you can. No matter what it is, this too shall pass. True freedom is to be one hundred percent okay with that. Today is a brand new day, and now is a brand new moment.

The difficulty with marriage

Almost every love story has the potential to begin as if it were a fairy tale. "Once upon a time, two people fell passionately in love and their love was unlike any others before theirs." Relationship beginnings are wonderful and the passion can experience a 'rebirth' with a wedding, honeymoon and the first year of marriage. Once a couple begins to grow and their lives change with jobs, children, social activities and other commitments, the love and romance become more difficult to attend to. Sometimes love and romance seem to be lost altogether. Most fairy tales do not end with "happily ever after."

In the movie Hector and the Search for Happiness, one of the items on his happiness list is the simple question "Does the person bring you predominantly (a) up or (b) down." Is your partner fighting mostly with, or for you? Do you love him or her enough to keep working on the love and romance? To whom are these relationship issues important, to you or someone else? I wrote about the differences between personality (attitude) and character in my Happiness book, in the context of professional networking. Let's use the same model in the context of a meaningful loving relationship. "Personality" is easiest to understand. Your personality is how people experience you. It's your public persona. But what is "character?" And why is it so crucial in a relationship? Character is who you are when no one is watching.

Let's think back again to the time you first fell in love. When the two of you met, you met each other's personalities. You showed your prospective partner your public persona, and you were shown their public persona. I'm not saying you tricked each other. How you display yourself to others is just your personality. But as the years go by you spend a lot of time together in close quarters, which makes it impossible to permanently sustain your public persona. Personalities eventually give way to an inner self that gets revealed for the first time. There you stand, naked as if no one is watching. But this time, someone is watching. And that's when you meet for the first time, all over again. It's another first date. This time it's a true meeting, a meeting of your characters. In many cases, you're not only meeting your partner, but you're meeting yourself for the first time. Most people don't recognize their own behavior, and wouldn't be caught dead treating anyone the way they treat their spouse. Maybe, at one point or another in your life, you've heard yourself say, or caught yourself thinking, "I'm just not myself with him/her." Then who is that person? That's you; it's your character.

One of the reasons many people fail at long-term relationships is not that they don't like their partner, it's that they don't like themselves. While everyone else in your life is a mirror reflecting your personality, your partner is a mirror reflecting your character. Most people are comfortable with their public persona, as they've invested time and energy in creating that persona. On the contrary, they don't like what they see when they're confronted with their own character, their true

> *"The difficulty with marriage is that we fall in love with a personality, but we must live with a character."*
>
> Peter de Vries

self. Judging by a climbing divorce rate, most of us would rather choose to be with someone else than remain with his or her spouse, and ourselves.

Marriage: a death at the altar

When we see someone we are attracted to, we project a future with that person, either positive or negative. Either way, we are not seeing that person as they are in that moment. In our projection we see a reflection of ourselves, as if we're looking into a mirror. The problem is, we believe our projection to be true already. Our projection becomes the framework in which we place the ideas we have about other people.

I'd be the first to admit that I'm a judgmental person, to a certain extent. As an author I project my ideas into books and believe they're true. When I meet you, I'll label you and place you in a box. It's how we make sense of the world. The problem isn't to label something, or believing that what I write is currently true for me. The problem is becoming rigid in your thinking. In his book Intuition, Malcolm Gladwell takes a very practical approach to those gut feelings and instincts that can guide us. In-tuition is a habit that can be learned. We're always looking externally for answers and guidance, ignoring the voice inside. Ignoring your intuitive signals will limit your potential in this world. Regardless of what your religious beliefs may be, I know guidance is available if you're open to it. It might just be those gut feelings and unexplainable emotions that transfer guidance from a higher power to your current reality. You have to be willing to silence the outside noise, and stop waiting for the big voice from the sky. Instead, learn to listen to the quieter one from deep inside.

If you could love someone on a scale from one to ten, whatever makes it a ten for you simply is what it is. You don't need to defend yourself to anyone. Opposites attract, they say. Quite literally, our partner is supposed to make up for everything we don't like about our past, present and future. We place so much value on compensating, that we might be willing to compromise and accept a relationship that is not appropriate or not working anymore. For example, let's imagine a relationship that has not worked for years. The couple is constantly arguing, sometimes even violently where voices are raised and things are said that can never be taken back. On top of that, they haven't slept together for years. Yet, when one of the partners leaves and maybe even goes off with someone else, the other partner who is left behind is devastated regardless. The upset is not because they lost their partner, but because they lost their projection of who that partner was to them. They lost their "better half", all those qualities they couldn't see in themselves but saw in their partner. No matter how non-existent or dysfunctional the marriage had become, they keep holding on to a distant memory of a relationship that died years ago.

In my Happiness book, I share the story about the candle ceremony:

The popular marriage ceremony where bride and groom light a bigger candle with their individual candles is something that goes against that model of individuality, and upsets me every time. Up until the point of lighting the candle I like the ceremony as a symbol of the life the couple creates together, but when they proceed by blowing out their individual candles, I check out. The lack of individuality and the idea everything has to be "we" now, is the main source for relationship issues, ultimately ending in separation and divorce. And it starts right at the altar, minutes after you say, "I do".

Traditional marriage is a funeral of absolute freedom. The model is beyond old fashioned, and while the romantic inside me appreciates the sentiment, reality is that marriage is reflective of something we used to do "in the old days" when women were not equal to men. Most of the legal system still in effect today, is based on that dated economic model. Most families are no longer made up of a patriarch figure putting bread on the table, with a matriarch figure nurturing and supporting the offspring. Why do we insist on basing the legal terms of our relationships on this model? In the Canadian province of Alberta, cheating on your lawfully wedded spouse is an offence punishable by jail time. Family laws are ancient. Is that archaic, economic model of marriage still valid in today's world? Haven't we moved on from the situation where men and women do not have any other choice?

> "Many people spend more time in planning the wedding than they do in planning the marriage."
>
> Zig Ziglar

Without freedom, there's no joy. True love, and friendship, should not need a legally binding contract, other than to protect you from those archaic models. While most family law is ancient and way past due for a modernizing update to make it more relevant, it often does leave room to write your own relationship code. Anything that's fixed and rigid is destined to fail eventually. Yet most of the people I've met in North America want to invest in the illusion of safety, security and predictability as early in life as possible. It's the polar opposite of what's happening in other parts of the world, where marriage is postponed until later, or doesn't happen at all. Have you seen much of the safety, security and predictability you're looking for lately? Or is marriage, in its traditional form, nothing more but a fantasy created by our insecure minds?

The Palace of Versailles

When I first announced I'm no longer a big believer in the institution of marriage, I knew I was committed to write this book. I do believe in long-term relationships more than anything else. The movie "Shall we Dance" describes it best for me.

Susan Sarandon, as her character Beverly Clark, describes the essence of being in a relationship, when she says:

> "There's a billion people on the planet… I mean, what does any one life really mean? But in a marriage, you're promising to care about everything. The good things, the bad things, the terrible things, the mundane things… all of it, all of the time, every day. You're saying 'your life will not go unnoticed because I will notice it. Your life will not go un-witnessed because I will be your witness."

I apply this quote to any committed romantic relationship. I consider it a privilege to have someone to witness what I'm doing with my life, and hold me accountable for going after my hopes and dreams. It puts a different spin on relationships, celebrating individuality while choosing to be together out of free will. With that freedom mindset, I believe the romantic odds significantly improve, and you might be together long enough to even celebrate the victories and successes in life, together. It doesn't have to be lonely at the top.

Balthasar Gracian wrote in his 17th century manual on success, The Art of Worldly Wisdom, as follows: "You are as much a real person as you are deep. As with the depths of a diamond, the interior is twice as important as the surface. There are people who are all facade, like a house left unfinished when the funds run out. They have the entrance of a palace but the inner rooms of a cottage." Reading the book reminded me of the Versailles house in one of Florida's gated communities. If and when construction completes, the house will be one of the largest and most expensive single-family homes in the United States. Construction started almost fifteen years ago, and it's still not finished. The owner, founder of a large timeshare company, ran into financial difficulty during the economic recession of 2008. The house has been called a monument to bad taste, but regardless of your opinion on real estate, it's the picture perfect example of an empty facade, with the interior still unfinished as this book goes to press.

Keeping your relationship alive goes hand-in-hand with developing the interior of your palace: personal growth and individual character development. If you want to improve one, you'll have to work on the other too. Taking a positive stance towards your life is what character is about. Having a zest for life, reigniting the fire of passion for doing the things you love. It takes more effort not to love, than to love. What would that mean for you? What passion have you left ignored for too long? What have you stopped doing without even realizing it? Love and passion are crucial. Happiness in my personal life at home is infinitely more important than happiness at work, even though I wrote a book on the latter topic first.

For many years I did everything I could to forget the past: expensive therapy, a library of self-help books, meditation, and even medication. I was actively resisting all the painful experiences from my past. The more I put my past behind me, the less effect it would have on me, I reasoned. But the more energy I directed towards my problems and pain, the more "stress" and "dis-ease" I continued to create in my life. There have been days I wish I didn't wake up in the morning. After recovering from a painful divorce, I was looking for a transition.

> *"I dislike the word 'self-help.' Self-awareness, yes, but not self-help."*
>
> Deepak Chopra

I wanted to attract a new relationship into my life. Instead I focused all my energy on holding on to my pain from the past. Life flows, but it doesn't always flow the way you want it to. I had to not only accept my reality, but deal with it, live it, and live with it. I couldn't blame anyone else for those circumstances. In rethinking and reframing my memories, I wanted to share my story as if the past didn't exist. I wanted to write this book of love without referring to the past, without admitting to my flaws and failures. But it doesn't work that way. Life repeats itself. You have to change your response to get a different outcome. As long as I continued to hold on to painful memories and limiting thoughts and beliefs, I continued to create separation. In the end I had to foot that bill myself. I didn't just create separation in my relationships, but essentially from my true self. I separated myself from love. I had to let go of the emotional pain of a break-up, past failures and the need for external approval. Thoughts like, "I'm not attractive" or "I will never have a loving relationship" didn't help. I had to consciously let go of those limiting beliefs. If you are your unique self, you will mature, grow and develop as a human being. You'll always be on an adventure, enjoying life. Some even say being authentic makes you younger. If you are mediocre and not living your truth you will feel unfulfilled and unhappy. I learned to live for the moment, and take things one day at a time. A day at a time was all that my depressed mindset could handle anyway. Embracing the moment became the cornerstone to escape my depressing reality and build an unlikely future. I committed to a year of transition, symbolized by planting a new tree in my backyard. Its growing roots became a visualization of me becoming more grounded every day as a person. I wasn't going to be the person I was expected to be anymore. I committed to have a good day, today, regardless of what my own plans for that day might have been. In order to make room for what you do want, you have to release and let go of the things you don't want. To attract what you want, you have to let go of everything that keeps you away from love. Live in the moment and let the rest of the world sort itself out. Commit to yourself: This is my life and I'm going for it.

Is your marriage a good marriage?

In an attempt to be polite, North Americans often don't say what they really mean. Being Dutch, I'm often too blunt and direct for their liking. When I was paying for my groceries the other day I signaled the cashier with my credit card I was planning to pay with plastic. She turned the debit machine towards me and said, "Whenever you're ready". Maybe it's because English is my second language, but it made me pause for a bit to reflect on her words. Too long apparently, because in the few seconds I took she got noticeably restless, gently took the card from my hand and swiped it for me. I guess, "whenever you're ready" doesn't really mean "whenever". The polite invitation had an unexpected expiry date after all. Sorry for missing the fine print.

There's more tricky fine print while shopping: I don't like, and avoid, anything that's free*. I don't mind free, the problem lies in the asterisk. The asterisk implies there's more to follow, often a laundry list of conditions that explain why I don't qualify for the offer, or why it's not really free to begin with. For example you might get a free hot tub, but you have to buy the million-dollar home first. Most times the fine print isn't even readable. It's like a radio commercial that quickly says, "conditions apply", and then the conditions are read out on-air, but so quickly it's impossible to understand what's being said, at least to this Dutch immigrant. Of course, the companies offering these unbelievable deals have to protect themselves from a legal perspective, because they're afraid of being sued (American companies) or taken advantage of (Canadian companies). I get that. No one can make a living by giving everything away for free, whether it's hot tubs, software, digital images, coffee, you name it. Unfortunately "free" doesn't pay the bills.

If married couples were as deeply in love as they are in debt from buying things with an asterisk beside it, life would be a whole lot easier. There are many marriages that are loaded up with debt from all the "happiness" vacations the couple has been on. In an attempt to reignite the passion, they overspent on a ticket as far away from reality as possible. I'm guilty as charged. I used to do all of that and more, but on my own. Looking back, I've done most of my soul-searching and self-discovery trips in Spanish speaking countries. I've always loved the Spanish language, and while I can keep myself alive when traveling through South America, I never made enough of an effort to actually learn the language properly. One of my New Years resolutions was to change that procrastinating behavior, so I set some goals towards becoming more proficient next time I visit Argentina. In one of the lessons, when learning new vocabulary related to people and family in our lives, the Spanish question that came up was "Es un bueno matrimonio?". It means, "Is it a good marriage?" It made me think. Is it? And what defines a good marriage?

The trend in North America is opposite from what I've seen in Europe. In North America, people get married at a younger age, then buy a small house, get a job, have kids, buy a bigger house, get a bigger job, have more kids and so on. The European trend that I witnessed before moving here was the exact opposite of that: you do everything else first, and then get married, maybe. Regardless of the sequence, I'm not a big fan of the institutionalized marriage anymore. It's not the commitment part I have an issue with, it's the institutionalization of it all: the "system" controlling your commitment as a couple. At the summit are the stag parties: one last night of freedom before it all ends. Weren't you committed already? What life changing difference does the marriage certificate make, if you need one more night of freedom? Is that the way to start a marriage, let alone a good one?

I haven't been invited to many stag parties, probably due to my reasoning above. I love a good party, but whenever I do attend one, the mandatory question always comes up from the groom-to-be: "so tell me, when are you getting married?" I try to dodge the bullet, because I feel sharing my true perspective on some guy's last night as a bachelor might ruin it all. I feel like a male version of Miranda in Sex and the City, telling Mr. Big that him and Carrie "are crazy to get married". I'm afraid I'll ruin the perfect wedding with that uncomfortable statement, leaving the prepaid honeymoon suite unoccupied. In the movie, the statement was made out of frustration over her own relationship. In my case, it has nothing to do with frustrations over the past, but with a different way of looking to the future. With divorce numbers on the rise, marriage should not be the popular thing to do anymore, despite the elusive "best day of your life"-dream that many girls (and boys alike) continue to hold on to. I've personally witnessed, and contributed to, a failing marriage. The legal system that created the institution of marriage is based on dated economic models. When couples fall apart, that very system works against the separation, keeping couples together in battle instead of moving along with their lives. Is buying in to a failing, outdated model with literally everything you own still the right thing to do? You're not supposed to point things like that out at a stag party, but at some point over half of married couples have to deal with it.

A committed, conscious relationship based on individual freedom means that two people choose to be together. It's a choice based on free will, not on a piece of paper someone external at church or city hall gave you. True love is the choice to stay together, while having the ability and independence to leave. The analogy might be inappropriate, however when I adopted my German shepherd dog I was afraid she would run for the hills if I let her off the leash. I kept her close by my side for the first few weeks after I adopted her, based on the trainers recommendation. However when I eventually was comfortable enough to let her off the leash, she never ran away. She stayed with me, right by my side as if I had never even taken the leash off. She has stayed right there ever since.

YOU

RECOMMITTING TO YOUR LIFE

Loving You

You have to think like an American. You'll feel so homesick that you'll want to die, and there's nothing you can do about it apart from endure it. But you will, and it won't kill you. And one day the sun will come out - you might not even notice straight away, it'll be that faint. And then you'll catch yourself thinking about something or someone who has no connection with the past. Someone who's only yours. And you'll realize... that this is where your life is.

Brooklyn

Escape from the greatest prison in life

The greatest prison you can live in is caring too much about what other people think. Other people are important, but to what extent are your happiness and wellbeing dependent on getting some form of approval from another person? So far in this book we've explored that question by looking at circles of other people in our life. We've worked our way inward, and built the foundation for an upgraded view to the way humans relate to each other. We've looked at the world, at coworkers and acquaintances, friends, family, and even your love one. In this final chapter it's time to go deeper, and look inside.

We live in an approval-addicted society, built around instant gratification. Social media has further developed our approval addiction, and removed true social connections. We share "selfies", and worry when not enough people "like" what we post. People are losing their ability to focus on what really matters. Living as an approval addict is like living in a mental prison. You have to constantly make sure you say the right thing, do the right thing, and create the right impression in order to get the much needed love and approval, and "likes" on social media networks. As a result, your feelings are on an emotional roller coaster all the time. Like a drug addict, you'll go from feeling the wonderful feelings that follow getting your approval fix, to the despair when your supply runs out.

Love and approval addiction are rooted in self-abandonment. Imagine the feeling part of you as a child. This is your inner child. When you are addicted to approval, you have handed your inner child away for adoption. Instead of learning to take responsibility for your own happiness by loving and approving of yourself, you have given your inner child away to others. You rely on them for love and approval, making those others responsible for your feelings. This inner self-abandonment causes the deep pain of low self-worth, making you dependent on others for your self-esteem and sense of worth.

Let's say your name is Christine. You are 34 years old. Inside you lives little Christine. She is, and always will be, about four years old. While you are busy doing a thousand things a day, mostly focused on taking care of other people, little Christine will feel neglected. You're exhausted every night from being always on the go to help others at home and at work. You make sure everyone's needs are fulfilled, except little Christine's. Sometimes she will throw a temper tantrum. You may feel angry at the world, more tired or even burned out, and wonder where it came from.

The worst feeling in the world is being disloyal and unsupportive to your self. To get out of that mental prison you have to become dissatisfied with your current situation first. If you're happy with where you are today it will be tough to break free. The first step towards change is awareness. Most of us have become complacent and comfortable at some point. To break free, we will need to work on our dissatisfaction with the faded life we're living. You'll have to work on your dissatisfaction with the person you have become, or are becoming. As long as you're not dissatisfied enough it will not outweigh the cost of the work and effort you'll have to put in. People will not suffer for no reason. Everybody has a price that has to paid, usually in advance. To move ahead from where you are today you'll need to start developing a vision for your life. Where are you today, where are you headed next, and, most importantly, why?

Getting past any addiction is a life long commitment. Any program you do or book you read to help beat the addiction is nothing more but a good place to start. That includes the one you're holding right now. The real work on beating the addiction starts after, once you've read the book or completed the program. In order to raise the level of the results you see in your life, you'll have to learn to raise your level of thinking. Focus on becoming a world-class thinker first, and a better version of you will unfold naturally. This requires a shift in perspective. The results you're looking for are for you personally, but the way to get there is to look to others. How can you make a difference in other people's life? What can you do to be of value to the other people in your life, in everything you do?

> "You have to go through those mountains and valleys - because that's what life is: soul growth."
>
> Wayne Newton

The path out of your "addict" comfort zone might not be easy. The minute you venture out of your comfort zone the emotions that have been running your life so far will raise all sorts of objections. Your brain is programmed to keep you safe, and within your comfort zone. Your mind will try to talk you out of venturing too far of the beaten path. To get past that initial point of hesitation, you'll need the right mental attitude and level of activity. I'm not talking about wishful thinking, which is synonymous for having a weak mindset. Delusion is the cancer of high performance. Without the right activities to confirm your attitude, the positive thinking by itself means nothing at all. To break free, you'll need to create a new vision for your life. You have to get out of your comfort zone in order to increase your comfort zone. It's like learning how to ride a bicycle, or motorcycle. Once you learn it, getting on the bike becomes second nature. Just like skiing, you need to go faster to maintain your balance. To make your turns easier, all you have to do is pick up a little speed, and let your equipment do the hard work for you. If you do it enough, and learn to let go, it almost becomes automatic. What do you have to lose by just living your life, without the need for constant external approval? What you go through doesn't matter, as long as you make it through.

The art of travel

What happened in the end? We're still alive. I'm still alive. After a few weeks of being apart we made it back together. Crisis is an excellent time for significant change to be realized. It's life's way of giving you leverage to manifest something new. Turning your goals into reality. Crisis is a shortcut to success. What is today could disappear any moment. If something like this happens for you, instead of feeling sorry for yourself, use the opportunity to take a deeper look at yourself. Your life is a unique and never to be repeated event. Open your mind, or someone will open it for you.

The loss of your life's partner, to death or them leaving, is a crisis. But reality is that unfortunately, eventually everyone will die, leave you, or otherwise go away. Until you stop resisting that fact, you won't experience true freedom. Freedom means having an awakening, as if you were standing outside your body, observing what's happening to you. Freedom means seeing the situation clearly for the first time. Freedom is the key to seeing yourself from a detached perspective. It's about being clear on why you're here. It's getting laser-focused on the direction towards reaching your ultimate goals in life. This final chapter is about getting clarity about what to do today in order to live your goals in reality. It'll answer three existential questions. First, how can you improve and do things in your life today, better. Second, how you can become clear on your values and what you really want out of life. Last, but not least: what is success in terms of love? Instead of describing portions of the elephant of absolute freedom, let's attempt to see the bigger picture for your life. If we were to meet three years from you reading this today, what has to have happened during that period for you to feel happy about your progress?

The art of travel is to deviate from one's plans. The best travel memories I have are from when something didn't go according to plan. Something extraordinary happened that I didn't expect, and it made all the difference. Most regrets in life are for things we didn't end up doing. In the top five regrets of the dying, many did not realize until the end of their life that happiness is a choice. They had developed comfortable patterns and habits for their life. This comfort zone of familiarity overflowed into their emotions, and eventually impacted their physical lives. A deep-rooted fear of change had them pretending to others, and to their selves, that they were content with the life they were living. All whilst deep within, they wished they had let themselves be happier. They longed to laugh properly and have silliness in their life again. The regret of not choosing happiness, unfortunately, is a surprisingly common one. What are the biggest opportunities you can focus on to seize the moment and achieve your goals in life? What are the biggest dangers you'll have to face and deal with, in order to achieve your progress? Take a fresh look at your life. See if you can disconnect from the stories of the past that hold you back. Maybe you'll develop a fresh way of seeing things, just as they are. There's no right or wrong, good or bad, allowed or not

> *"Let yourself be silently drawn by the strange pull of what you really love. It will not lead you astray."*
>
> Rumi

allowed, possible or impossible. I'm asking you to look, really look at your life, and start loving you by re-identifying with who you really are.

If you were commissioned as an artist to paint a picture of an effective, joyful, harmonious way of living, what would that look like? Would you have designed your life the way you are living it today? For every goal you have today, what experience will it bring to your life? Answer this question honestly, but quietly for yourself. The answer will reveal your passion, and underneath your passions you'll discover your true values. The goal is to dream as big as you want, not smaller or bigger based on what your environment might say or think. If you did not refer to the past, or your conditioning, or the way you used to look at life, how would you design your life today? What is an intelligent way to live your life? Do you spend your time doing something that you do not want to be doing? What strengths will you need to reinforce and maximize? What skills and resources do you need to develop to capture the opportunities in front of you? If you dare to be honest with yourself, your heart already knows the answer. The quiet voice inside you will not lead you astray. Allow yourself to forget all practical considerations. I grant you full permission to be you.

There is nothing wrong with building a life in our modern world, even if that means looking for outside fulfillment for now. You need that outside fulfillment to make life bearable and less boring. Be gentle with yourself. There is no such thing as wrong. But like a drug, outside fulfillment does not last forever, let alone bring inner fulfillment. The one thing that connects us all as human beings is that we're all unique. Uniqueness is what makes humans beautiful. We are here to be our own unique self. If we are overly influenced by anybody or anything else, and are addicted to external approval then we reduce ourselves to living a mediocre and boring life. We have enough people in that stage on the planet already. In this chapter, I invite you to challenge yourself to be more. I want you to go further and faster, with less effort. Taking action is required, and hard work may be required as well. Yet, struggling doesn't have to be part of the deal. You don't have to work so hard to be perfect. All you have to do is consider the possibility that what you really want is possible. What's the next thing that would have to happen to make that dream a reality?

When I went skiing on a very cold day last season, I rode the gondola up the mountain with a guy who was full of stories. I never asked for his name, but let's call him Robert. One of the stories he told was about his friend who had nearly died in a hiking accident due to an unexpected snowstorm. As he was telling the story, I expected the worst and thought his friend surely had passed in that unfaithful event, but the story continued. While he made it through that accident alive, he died a few years later in a plane crash. The two events seemed so unrelated it was almost humorous. But Robert concluded the story saying that his friend wasn't confident enough flying the small planes: "I've flown a few myself, and even though I'm no expert, I felt more confident myself than when I saw my friend fly one." When we reached the top, he said one more thing with a sincere sense of urgency, "go confidently in the direction of your dreams".

Writing your own life story

This week I was waiting on the phone with the customer service department of a company I had ordered something from that never showed up. Over and over again, I thought of things I could have done while I sat there, waiting, not living my life, listening to music I didn't even like. Are you "on hold" in your life? Are you waiting for a spouse to come along, or for him or her to act better towards you? Are you waiting for the motivation to get your home organized? Are you waiting for a great job to fall into your lap? Are you waiting for winning the lottery to plan your retirement?

Eighty percent of your problems come from twenty percent of your life. Determine what the small percentage is that's affecting so much of your life, and start working towards making it happier, more efficient, and more satisfying. You're always looking for something out there, something that you haven't seen yet. The biggest secret is that what you're looking for isn't something out there. It's something that you carry with you every day. You already have what it takes to be free, and successful. As we near the end of this book I'll share some ideas to help get unstuck, and get going again. Let's get started.

It starts with love. First, let go of all your past negative attitudes and limiting beliefs. Then, choose to love your life, every minute of every day. Love everything that happens to you, and make each moment a real part of your life. Love your car, your house, the trees and the flowers. Love the birds and appreciate the beautiful sounds they make. Love your friends and love your neighbors. Love is a state of mind. You can just decide to do it, and when you do, you will find that love bounces back to you, and with it the ability for you to work wonders with your mind. Get used to this new way of feeling and it will lift your experiences in life.

Love is one of the secrets to attract good things back to you. It starts with you. You, as a person, are unconditionally loved. There's nothing you can do wrong. You can do good, and do well at the same time. There's no need for limiting "either/or"-thinking. You can love every minute of the day and make it a real part of your life. Your passion and purpose are overlapping. Once you allow yourself to take action and choose in favor of your passions you'll discover what it means to feel alive. Your life's purpose can be broad or very specific. Your purpose can be the full image covering every detail, or simply the next step to take. You're born with a set of qualities and talents, and your purpose in life is to make that shine in everything you do. But what is the difference between those who are successful at that, and those who are not? "I want to be someone who helps others" could mean anything, from a barista in a coffee shop to a heart surgeon. Focus on who you want to be. Be as specific as possible. And then stop waiting, and take action. The only difference between you and the so-called "successful" people, who are getting what they want, is that they took massive action, and kept moving.

Look at your life today. Do you find yourself watching endless hours of television? Are you trying to escape emotional and spiritual pain by taking drugs or alcohol? Do you indulge in overeating to still an emotional hunger? What distractions take you out of being present with what you are feeling? For me, constant travel was the perfect way to take me away from a life I didn't like in the first place. It didn't matter where I was; I took myself along with me for the ride. Bottled up pain and emotions I hadn't dealt with were there all along with me, affecting my body and energetic space. The few days or weeks away always did me good. While I was travelling, I felt happier, and more engaging. I felt less disconnected from my true self, my purpose, and my story.

What's the story of your life? At what time did you feel happiest? I ask authors in my book-writing program: What's the most meaningful story you have to tell the world? Your life is made up of a chain of similar stories that somehow link together. Regardless of whether you classify each story as a success or failure, it's just a story. Your life's story is a story you own and carry with you everywhere you go. No matter how far you venture away from home, you'll always bring yourself with you. In your luggage you carry the entire weight of your collection of stories. The weight of a story is made up of the feelings and emotions you've added to the story: the fear, anger, sadness, happiness, and every other emotion associated with that story. Until you decide to let those emotions go, you'll have a heavy backpack to carry. One way of letting go is forgiving yourself. You can choose to let go of the blame and negative emotions associated with the stories of the past. Everything else will take care of itself.

> *"We all have a life story and a message that can inspire others to live a better life or run a better business."*
>
> Brendon Burchard

We all have experienced or learned something significant in life. We all have a story that, when shared, will be of value to the world. But instead of sharing our story, we compare ourselves to others. This kind of jealousy causes self-disgust. Comparing is the fastest way to feel inferior and lose our self-esteem. We forget about the benefits of what we've learned in the process. Comparing creates separation. Everybody struggles his or her own battles but that doesn't make your story any less important. Do not think anyone else is better or worse than you. Making comparisons can spoil your happiness. In comparing our story to others, we fail to see we're on our own unique path. Your life is a unique, never to be repeated event. Instead of comparing your story to others, write it down. I help budding authors get past that blank page, and give them a structure to put the story they own down on paper. It's a powerful process. Something they'll say will have the power to change somebody's life. Maybe not the entire story, but a piece of it. That's the basic concept my book writing course is based on. Just like that, at least a small piece of your story will resonate with what someone else is going through right now, in his or her own way.

Everyone has a story to share that not only deserves to be heard, it's your moral imperative to get it out there. Not sharing your life lessons, keeps that experience locked up in your mind. Nobody can benefit from it there. In not going after what you really want, who are you letting down? Not only are you letting yourself down, but who else? Who in your environment are you not supporting by not going after your dream? As I tell my authors, the goal is not to replicate Shakespeare, as that would be another bad comparison to make. The goal is to get your story out of your head, and down on paper. Only when your story is written down it has the impact to touch somebody else's life, and help them on their unique path. Chances are it will not be the book in it's entirety that'll change someone's life, it'll be that one paragraph, or even one sentence, that'll give someone a new viewpoint, make them think, and ultimately help them along on their journey. By not sharing your story, not writing your book, you'll never write that one sentence that has a significant, beneficial impact on somebody else.

Is it time to get started on your story, and write it down? Whether you decide to publish your life story in a book, or just talk more about what truly matters at the water cooler at work, you have a choice in what to share. Sharing your story helps you letting go those painful memories from the past that will block your growth. The past isn't fixed. Telling your story will help you reframe the limiting beliefs you've been holding on to in your life. You're no longer the person you used to be. You can focus on what parts of the story you share, and how. The story is about the core of your life, the things you build your life around that matter. It might just be that one sentence, but it'll make a difference to someone.

Rethinking fear

As a baby we're only born with two fears: the fear of falling, and the fear of loud noises. All other fears are learned behaviors that we introduced to our mind at a later age. And it's exactly those fears that are limiting the amount of love and happiness we can experience in life. Everything you want in life is outside your comfort zone, on the other side of fear. Deep down we're searching for the same thing. We have all been conditioned and programmed from the day we were born, and the environment we're in is constantly reinforcing all the conditioning from the past. If our mind encounters an event that doesn't fit one of the labels we've learned, the natural response is a feeling of fear. It can be something big or small, but the root feeling is the same. Fear is your minds way of keeping everything unknown out. Your mind believes that's how it keeps you safe, and to an extent, it does. You'll comfortably stay in your comfort, or mediocre zone, if you choose to believe the current thoughts you think and the feelings you feel. It's like a bad relationship: it's not bad enough to leave, but is it good enough to stick around? You have to be willing to venture out of that comfort zone in order to achieve success and greatness in your own life. If you want something different in life, and grow beyond your current comfort zone, you can use the tricks your mind plays on you to your advantage. You can learn to welcome and embrace fear. That doesn't mean you have to get unnecessarily uncomfortable. Outside your comfort zone doesn't mean you have to stretch all the way to your panic zone. We've all been there. You can still learn from that experience too, but learning is optimized when you're somewhere on the happy median between your comfort zone and your panic zone. Be gentle with yourself. Don't ignore fear, but figure out what the story is behind the fear. Make a different choice if you wish. Duality is a core operating principle of our mind, but there is another level beyond what we are trained to observe. Your mind is nothing more but a big filing cabinet, which contains things that both support and not support you. Neutralize the old, non-supportive thoughts and enhance the supportive thoughts. Change comes with joy and purpose, not with anger and fear.

Finding and following your passion in life helps you move forward, but you can have too much of a good thing. Loving my job and being passionate about the work I do, means I have lost sight of the other areas of life at times, which are equally important. It's not just the popular duo of work versus life. Humans are holistic beings. You cannot impact one area of your life without impacting others. While we occupy our minds with the duality of rights versus wrong, the universe only knows a holistic balance versus imbalance. True happiness is finding the delicate balance in all areas of life, all of them being equally fulfilling and contributing to your overall happiness.

> *"Sometimes losing balance for love is part of living a balanced life."*
>
> Eat Pray Love

People have often told me, "Your life looks pretty good". While I'm grateful for the things I've been able to accomplish thus far, I never thought of my life that way. I'm always working towards something new, and tend to under appreciate where I am today. This can make spending any significant amount of time with me a bit of an exhausting experience. Myself included: I over-lived my passion. You can still burn yourself out, even if you spend your time doing what you love. Awareness is always the first step to change. You cannot change something if you're not even aware it needs to be changed. You need to understand where your programming and mental patterns come from, in order to deconstruct them and create a new reality. If you don't like something about your life, you have to take ownership and look in the mirror. Recondition your mind. Rethink the way you think. Be willing to do the unsexy things nobody else wants to do. If living the dream was easy everybody would be doing it. We live in a world of cause and effect. Everything you experience is a result. It's like the butterfly effect: if you say that you've tried something before and it didn't work, try changing the slightest, smallest detail as it might create an entirely different outcome.

If you get too comfortable the universe will give you a lesson to show that what you're doing is not good for you. Resistance to those lessons is futile. They keep repeating themselves until you get the message. There's no such thing as a missed opportunity. Eventually the same lesson will present itself again, allowing you to make a different choice if you wish. The bigger the lesson, the bigger the fear you'll feel and the crisis you'll experience. Finding true freedom is not an easy process, but the best way out is through. When my life fell apart in the fall of 2015, the first person I questioned was myself. I had to get off my high horse. I had to get over myself once again. For once I didn't have to fight for what I wanted, but for who I wanted. I had a choice as to where my life would go next, and opted to let go of everything else in order to survive. What you resist persists. I didn't want to be a victim then, and today I hope my story can be of benefit to you. You always have a choice. The key to living a happy life is making every decision in favor of your true passions. Take one step at a time and move forward despite the internal or external pushback and objections. To do that, I had to accept the good and the bad. Accepting life includes allowing negative emotions to be there and have their place. There's nothing I've seen about greatness that's conventional. Greatness is by definition unconventional. In order to succeed you have to dare to take that first step out of your comfort zone. If you're not exactly where you want today, you have to work on your belief system. Right now, how is your belief in you?

No problem or situation is permanent if you're taking massive action to resolve it. In one of my darkest days, I wrote on my bathroom wall, "even if this is all I can do, I'm going to f*ing do it now". Responsibility equals accountability, and accountability equals control. If you want to have any success in your life you have to take control of that life through responsibility and accountability. Look in the mirror, instead of pointing fingers. Don't go through life with a victim mentality. Own it all: the good, the bad, the ugly, and then get to work. If not now, when? If you're committed to carry it through to the end, you'll witness your life growing to another level. Taking full control of your life is the most liberating thing you can do. True freedom can only be experienced when you're in control.

Stay true to your personal mission

Your ongoing personal development and finding daily inspiration are both keys to a successful, and happy life. It's about the core of your life, the things you build your life around that matter. If you want to feel fulfilled you'll need to understand what makes you tick. The core should always be built on a foundation of joy. What would really make you happy? Most successful businesses have an unusual clarity about what they've set out to accomplish. Have you ever asked yourself that question? Once you know the answer to your intrinsic why, obstacles don't matter anymore. Your why is the foundation of your personal mission statement, and becomes the fuel that helps you get to meet and exceed your goals. By leveraging the power of intention, having a mission statement will bring you one step closer to your goals.

Every successful business has a well-defined mission statement. Writing one for yourself is a great way to make it known to yourself and others where you envision yourself to be. When you are clear about your goals you can be constantly working towards them. Without it, you might have a sense of direction, but no idea what the destination will be. Many people go through life on autopilot without a clear destination in mind, and wonder why they never achieve their goals and dreams. A navigation system like the one you might have in your car can help you head in general north direction, but it works much better if you enter an exact street address as a destination. Your mental navigation system works the same way. If you don't want to be the kind of person who passively lets things happen to them, a personal mission statement is what will help you program your internal navigation system. If you want to get where you are going in life you can start writing yours today.

All you need to get started on your personal mission statement is a pen and a piece of paper. Sit down and write about the person you are today. Do you like yourself? Do you like your life? Do you think that there are areas in your life that you could improve? Write about yourself and your life in a positive way. If you were living the life of your dreams, what would it look like? How would you change the different areas of your life for the better? Focus on your strengths and your abilities. Write how you want to change and in what areas of your life. Write about the goals that you want to see yourself meet over time. This may take some time, but I challenge you to be honest with yourself and design the life of your dreams.

Your personal mission statement is not a wish list of things that you want to possess. What you want the most is often not a set of materialistic things. Even though those might be the first you think about when you ask yourself what you truly want. Things and possessions are perfectly wonderful dreams, but an indication of a deeper desire for a feeling, or an experience. Experience is fuel for your body and your system. What do you choose to fuel your system with? Try to capture the feelings and experiences you're longing for to understand your intrinsic why. The most powerful mission statement is about being of service: giving those feelings and experiences back to the world and your loved ones. Your mission statement will help you to find your place in the world, and what you can be doing for those around you. Take your time writing it, making being of service to others your main focus. Your statement has the power to change your entire life for the better by giving it not just direction, but destination.

For many years I pretended to be more conservative than I really was. To get started on my mission statement meant I first had to give myself permission to let go of all guilt, as well as the resistance associated with that guilt. I had to let life be, and let it happen. Instead of pretending to be many things that I was not, I had to commit to being me. If I continued to worry about what everybody else was doing and thinking, how was I supposed to grow as a person? I decided, regardless of the outcome, to truly live my life. I committed to being me, and really go for it, no matter what "they" would say or think about me. To change the course of my life, I had to shut out the outside noise, get quiet and focus on what I really wanted. When things get dark and hard the default reaction is to hide in the confines of our comfort zone. There we wait, do nothing, and hope the situation will sort itself out. But does the book you're looking for fall miraculously off the shelf? Does that call from the person you need just come? Miracles happen, but you have to take action. I committed to take massive action.

> *"Whenever you find yourself on the side of the majority, it is time to pause and reflect."*
>
> Mark Twain

You'll never make it

I'm a big believer in setting goals and priorities. My Happiness book has an entire section dedicated to setting goals and finding better ways to achieve them. Setting firm, daring goals and having the right priories in place are key ingredients to make dreams become a reality. But the world isn't flat. Once you made it all the way to the horizon, the realization of your dream, it's not the end of the world. Most people give up long before they even reach the finish line, or stop right when they reach it. Somewhere along the way their mind talked them out of continuing the pursuit. Don't stop, neither when you reach the finish line, nor before it. To reach your goals, keep going and always stay in motion. Those that persevere, discover more beyond the imaginary horizon we placed our goal on. Be present in each moment, ready to experience new things. Lessons are all over the place if you are willing to look for them. You're never done learning. You've never made it.

When writing and editing this book, certain ideas and chapters didn't make it into the final version because we didn't like them and decided to throw them out. They didn't fit as well with the rest of the book as I thought they originally would. In creating and writing your life story the same model applies. We often look up to celebrities and people we think have "made it". We compare our story, the story we know in full, to their story, which we only know the best parts of. If we were to look closer, we would see that those celebrities all have their own battles to fight and issues to deal with. The pedestal we've placed them on only exists in our perspective of what we think is their reality.

I've met my share of influential people, and without exception they all have their challenges to deal with, just like us "normal people". The difference is that the people we think have "made it" don't choose to give too much attention to the less positive parts of their story. They focus on their successes, and accomplishments. We can choose to do the same thing when we share our story. We can choose to highlight the things we're proud of and excited about. Even if there is someone you admire, use him or her as a model to improve yourself. Fight for what you need to fight for. What you want to fight for is going to be different for everyone. We all have our own goals. You may think the definition is the same, but one of the reasons most people struggle, especially in relationships, is because the goal is different for everyone. You have to be willing to accept that you don't know it all. The more open to learning and coaching you are, the faster you will reach your goals.

When you direct your energy to positive areas, you'll change your mindset to become more positive about your life. Subconsciously you'll start to believe in yourself again. We're often our own worst enemy, and deal with a lot of negative self-talk. We make ourselves believe we're not good enough or will never go very far in life. If we choose to feed our subconscious mind positive stories and thoughts about our life, it will eventually start to change the tone of the feedback it gives us, and our internal critic becomes an internal guide.

As a quick exercise, pick any celebrity that you look up to, and see how their accomplishments line up with your own. It doesn't matter how insignificant you think the resemblance might be. If you can recognize their success, it means that inside your own being you hold that same trait of success and happiness. If you didn't own that success already, you wouldn't be able to recognize it in others either. Instead of focusing on the gap between their accomplishments and yours, focus on the level of achievement you've already accomplished. Celebrate your successes. In comparing yourself to others, we always tend to get the short end of the stick. That's fine to create contrast and get more clarity on where you want to go, but it's even more important to focus on the similarities instead of solely on the differences. Concentrate on what you already have accomplished, instead of what you haven't yet.

As a photographic artist, I remember selling my first artwork. It was a moment of significance, a small victory to be celebrated and remembered. It happened at an outdoor market, under my white canopy. It had taken me weeks of preparation to get ready for that event. I had bought and rented everything I needed to put together my little shop for that day, under that white tent. It was a lot of work, and I remember thinking that having a physical store or gallery somewhere down the road would be a nice achievement. I would have definitely "made it" once that dream would become a reality.

Sometimes dreams are closer than we think. It took me less than a year to get my very own retail location, albeit temporary. By now my work has been in featured in art galleries, too. As much as I enjoyed and celebrated those experiences, I never got a feeling that I had "made it". The unique experiences were worth the tremendous efforts, but in the end of the day it was just another project involving a ton of work. Instead of something that seemed a destination, it turned out to be another stepping stone on the journey of my artistic career. By now I've given up on the idea of "making it". There's always more beyond the horizon. Like me, I don't think you'll ever "make it", because you already have. The difference lies in the realization there's always something to do next, whatever that may be. You already have what it takes. It's like driving a car during nighttime. The headlights will only reach so far, and what's beyond the reach of our high beams we don't know. Yet we can make it all the way across the country by just seeing the next little bit of our path in front of us. As Martin Luther King said, "You don't have to see the whole staircase, just take the first step."

Taking control of your life

You can't control world politics, but you can vote. You can't control natural disasters, but you can be prepared in your own home. You can't control the construction crews on the highway, but you can control how much time you allow for your daily commute. Knowing what you can control and exercising that, and letting go of what you can't, puts you in the driver's seat of your life. There is only one person who is fully responsible for your life: you. Finding happiness within starts with acceptance of your self, as well as your circumstances and situations. Life will never be perfect. But life gets more perfect the second you're willing to accept that it's not. Happiness comes when you accept the imperfection, the flaws, the ups and downs, and enjoy the moments in life. All we really have is the now, so let's commit to enjoying it: celebrating and enjoying our time on planet earth.

If we want to be successful in life, we first have to take total responsibility for that life. We're responsible for all our successes and failures, health, relationships, financial situation, our feelings and everything else. You have created the life you're living today. You have take full responsibility for your creation. Only by taking responsibility, you put yourself in the driver's seat to achieve things that are important to you and change your life for the better. To take full responsibility, we must stop blaming others for our problems and failures. We have created our current situations by our thoughts and activities so there is no reason to blame anybody. We can only blame ourselves, but that is also useless because the past is the past; we can't change it. But now we can use this knowledge to create our future and get the results we want. This is based on Jack Canfield's formula: E+R=O (Event + Response = Outcome). The formula says that every outcome we experience in life (good or bad) is the result of how we responded to an event in our lives. Taking one hundred percent responsibility means you've promoted, created, or allowed something to happen. That includes love and relationships. Act as if you had complete control of the situation, and you might find a clue on how to improve it, no matter how unsatisfying reality is today. Even if people are pushing your buttons, it's a gift to realize you are the one that has those buttons. You have the ability to do something about it.

In similar situations, people react differently. Using the same information and circumstances some people are successful, others are not. By responding in a different way, they get different results. Trying to change the event that we blame for our failure is often impossible. Instead, consider changing your response to the event in order to get the results you're after. We can change our thinking, our behavior, and our communication. We can also change old habits into new, better ones. You'll have to give up all blaming, complaining, and other negative responses you've been holding on to. Even though complaining might lead to self-justification, it ultimately doesn't bring you the success you're after. Instead of complaining, consider how you can create a different reality by changing something small in what you're doing today. If you don't like the relationship you're in today, either leave or stop complaining.

Adopting a loving mindset has the power to bring you bigger and better results. Freedom starts with cultivating a loving heart to reach the perpetual motion of success. Success is about sharing from the heart. Giving praise, teaching others, sharing your advice, and educating from your experiences, are just a few examples. Once you set the flow in motion, success brings more success. Success, like change, begins with awareness, and then taking the next step. You have to be willing to accept a certain degree of risk. Be patient and be courageous. A better world starts by looking in the mirror. If your mind is preoccupied with negative thoughts, like anger, fear, and hatred, you'll slow down, stop or even reverse your progress. And that undesirable end result once again started with you.

Life is not meant to be perfect, nor is it meant to be easy. Life is a game. You are the player. In any sports game, the players pride themselves in their ability to beat challenges. They overcome obstacles. Nobody said it would be easy, just that the journey would be worth it. As a human species we constantly look for challenges to get through, whether it is getting to the top in our career, buying a car, owning a house, moving to another country, having a kid and then another kid, starting our own business, investing in businesses, learning another language, or doing a triathlon. We look for challenges for the sake of overcoming them. Even though a perfect life might sound ideal, I would get bored very quickly if there were no challenges left to overcome, with no lessons left to learn. Life has its own flow that has to take its course. The key is to find your natural self and do what you're good at in the middle of it all.

You already have what it takes

If I can do it, you can do it, but will you? In setting goals, or admiring those of others, most people just talk about taking action. Goals without action are nothing but a nice dream. Life is not about what you say, but about what you do. Talking about moving to a different continent at a birthday party is something entirely different from actually going ahead and doing exactly that. Many talk about it, but when you actually make the move you might end up living a lonely existence. Are you willing to do what it takes to create the reality you want in your life? The stars never align, timing will never be perfect and there will always be something to hold you back or stop you. I don't care about what you say or about what you think. I care about what you do. Watch yourself next time your mind comes up with a story about why not.

We are able to achieve whatever our minds can conceive and believe. There's a universal law that won't allow you to dream a dream if you didn't have it in you to accomplish that very dream. Henry Ford said, "Whether you think you can, or you think you can't - you're right." That makes it your moral imperative to replace all your negative expectations with positive ones. Only by taking the goal of finding freedom as an absolute, your mind can start to work towards the exact outcome you want, or something even better.

People often do not reach their goals, not because they lack required skills, but because they don't believe they can reach them.

Most people, who ever accomplished anything in life, had no idea about how they were going to do it. Many of them didn't have a college degree on their wall. They didn't have decorative letters or university titles surrounding their names. They just believed that the work they did had to be done, regardless of the outcome. Not doing the work they believed in was not an option, and they found a way to make it possible. Despite setbacks, they continued to believe in the importance of their mission and their ability to make it happen. They took control by taking responsibility, and realized that if they wanted to create the great and successful life they desired, they had to believe they could make it happen. They felt a sense of urgency behind the work they were doing. That sense of urgency is lacking from most modern day passions. Encouraging anyone to follow their dream is pointless if they don't believe themselves it's their duty and birthright to get that meaningful work done. We've become complacent, being all too comfortable within the mediocre zone of our mind's conditioning. Do you care enough about your goals and dreams to treat them with urgency? You have to believe that you have all the abilities, skills and inner resources to accomplish exactly what you've set out to do. Believing that you can achieve whatever you set your mind on is a choice you can commit to. If, even if deep down on some level, you think that something is impossible to achieve, you're probably not going to find the motivation or energy to overcome all obstacles and make it happen. At some point your mind will talk you out it, possibly with the finish line and everything that lies beyond in sight. Negative words and thoughts have a negative and limiting influence. On the other hand, if you believe that it is possible to achieve a goal that's important to you, you'll do everything necessary to achieve it. To be free we have to give up any sentence that starts with "I can't". Freedom means believing in yourself and daring to go after your dreams. Your brain has enough power to solve any problem you give it and help you reach any goal you have. You will make it happen.

Your core essence, also known as your authentic self, has a deeper, intrinsic reality. Unlike your ego-based identity, your core existence does not depend on external approval or stories we tell about ourselves. Unlike your ego, your authentic self does not feel threatened by someone else's success, or improved by their failure. Competition is good, but compete with nobody but yourself. At your core level everyone has the ability and resources to do abundantly well. You can visualize your ego-identity as the surface of the ocean. While you can see the movement of the water, you can't see everything that goes on underneath. Like the water, your identity is changeable and vulnerable. It reflects the sun, sky, and clouds, and is affected by whatever direction the wind blows from. Your authentic self is the vast, calm, still, deep water underneath the surface. Those deep mysterious waters hold your true potential. Even though much of what goes on is not visible from the outside, the potential is as real as the surface you can see. And whether you realize it or not, all that potential is already there.

All personal growth and transformation involves a process of diving deeper, underneath the surface. Just like deep-water diving, this process involves being uncomfortable in unfamiliar surroundings. Your identity is shaken out of its apparent solid form. Like ocean waves, it's forced to expand and reflect a deeper level of reality underneath. Training your identity to align itself with the voice of your authentic self takes practice. The ego doesn't exist, and therefore doesn't have to be defended or suppressed. Your identity is just a perspective, and you can choose to change the perspective you have about yourself. By loving your authentic self, you can transform your self-image. Once you get clear on your mission, you can use the power of your identity for the purpose it was created in the first place. It'll allow you to take an upgraded view towards love in all your relationships. Love expresses the unlimited potential of your core essence, and fulfills your purpose here on earth.

You need to first love yourself, they say. But what does that mean? Often we do much more for others than we do for ourselves, forgetting to take care of ourselves completely along the way. While selflessness seems to be the right thing to do, if you're not taking care of yourself you will also decrease your ability to take care of others. In anything you do, be of service to others and leave every situation better as you found it. If you can show the benefit for others in what you have to offer, people will be able to apply what you're saying to their own life and see what problems you can solve for them. Approval addiction is holding us back in life. Most people make others responsible for their feelings and do not take good care of their inner self. They think having goals and dreams for their own life is selfish and self-indulgent. They forget that only when we do take care of ourselves in the ways that we need to, we are truly capable of being of service to someone else. I have found taking care of yourself to be even more important when you're away from "home" and from your usual, familiar support systems. When traveling for extended periods, and especially when living abroad permanently, there are many new

> *"Whether you think you can, or you think you can't– you're right."*
>
> Henry Ford

and unfamiliar things to learn and take care of. In the midst of it all, it is easy to forget to take care of you. I worked myself past the point of burnout several times after moving to Canada. It happens to us all at one point or another, to various degrees.

Feeling good about yourself will come naturally when you stop waiting and start creating the life you really want to live. Stress and frustration will be reduced as you make choices instead of being pushed around based on other people's opinions. Loving yourself is building a strong inner connection with you. You'll experience a higher sense of self-acceptance. The process of self-improvement you'll undergo along the way will become easier and easier. True self-care starts by loving the truest version of yourself you know. Treat your self like a loving parent would do with their child. It's about not giving your inner child, and all it's feelings, away for adoption. Instead, learn how to truly take care of your inner child, including all it's wants and needs and occasional temper-tantrums. Protect the six inches in between your ears. What you focus on expands. Focus on your accomplishments and the things you can control instead of comparing yourself to others. By comparing you only notice the things you didn't do yourself. When you focus on what's not working and what you're struggling with, that is what expands, and as a result you'll experience more of the things you don't want in your life. It takes practice and mental toughness to maintain that focus on progress without getting sidetracked. If you can master your focus you'll be ready for anything. What other people say or think of you doesn't matter so much anymore, if at all.

Things are different now

Are you sitting on the fence of change? You're there because the path you've been on hasn't been working. If you want to change your life you must first change your mind. There are no solutions when you only focus on the negative, so instead of dwelling on the things that are going wrong in your life, take a step back and be thankful for the good things that are happening in it. Give change a chance, you can always climb back over. Change may seem scary until you look back at your past and realize how grateful you are.

It's not the situation that is challenging. It's your own expectations and assumptions that create the trouble. It's easier to hold on past conditioning than to ask the hard questions about the ideas you thought supported you. "Blanket beliefs" are not accurate nor are they useful as guidelines. When you take a step back you'll realize that many of those limiting beliefs and fears are only true some of the time. Love comes in many different forms, not always in big gestures but in small acts of kindness towards yourself and others. Most times you are good enough, someone is listening to you and people are willing to change.

Live your life with a philosophy. Thanks to our information age, there are so many resources available that will help you accomplish almost anything, whether it's losing weight, quitting smoking, or writing a book. Success leaves clues. There's no need to reinvent the wheel. Chances are somebody has already done what you're trying to accomplish. Despite all those resources available at your fingertips, there are fewer and fewer people following the plan. Change takes time, and along the way you might get the sense that everything you have been trying isn't working at all. Reality is that you probably haven't been doing it long enough. You haven't focused on the goals of your new reality long enough to see them materialize. You have to set your priorities and spend your time in alignment with the goals you've set. You'll see more changes over time, and as you learn and grow you'll make less and less mistakes. Too many people think they're so far away from their goals, and yet they are so close. Stop fighting against anything you might perceive as bad in your life. We all know someone who knows someone who has been fighting hard against cancer and lost that battle. How come we don't fight as hard for our life and win - while we can?

> *"People wait all week for Friday, all year for summer, all life for happiness"*
>
> *Unknown*

A mirror through which we look at ourselves is nothing more but a piece of glass with a silver lining. When we approach life through that silver cover, all we are able to see is ourselves. Discard the cover, and you will be able to see and feel everyone else as well. That's love. In life, look at your self in the mirror with love and care. A mirror reflects only us; a window is the door to compassion, health and true wealth. Don't let the mirror distract you from life, the people you love, and those who need your support.

Lighten up. Live a little. You're awesome. Have fun. Don't worry so much about what others think. You'll be fine. I love you. And as always, I wish you a *bon voyage* for the best journey of your life.

Parting words

In true Freedom Project tradition, at the end of the book I want to include some inspiring words written by someone else. This story has been shared online, and the author is unknown to me. It's about someone who went to see the neighborhood Rabbi to ask for advice about finding his or her true way in life.

The rabbi took me to the window. "What do you see?" he asked me.

Promptly, I answered, "I can see people walking to and from and a blind man is begging for alms at the left corner."

The Rabbi nodded and guided me to a big mirror. "Now look and tell me what you see?"

"I can see myself," I man answered.

The Rabbi smiled. "Now you can't see anyone else. The mirror and the window are both created from the same raw material: glass, but because on one of them they have applied a thin layer of silver, when you look at it all you can see is your own reflection."

The Rabbi placed his arm on my shoulders. "Compare yourself to those two pieces of glass. Without the silver layer, you saw the other people and felt compassion for them. When you are covered with silver, you see only yourself."

I looked at the Rabbi and stared. "I don't understand."

The Rabbi continued. "You will become someone only if you have the courage to remove the silver covering over your eyes in order to again see and love others."

He patted me on my back and sent me on my way.

Wait... there's more!

Looking forward to getting into action after reading The Freedom Project? Maybe you're not yet sure on where to get started, or maybe you already have some ideas as to what you would like to do, but could use some support along the way.

You'll find many other Freedom Project resources, online training, events and much more on the web page of this book. Nothing changes as much as the world of the internet, so to prevent me from including a collection of links that might no longer work in future, I'm adding these next few pages as a place to start and explore from there. Start by visiting the web page of this book:

www.freedomprojectbook.com

Please stay in touch with the Freedom Project community. My blog and magazine Living by Experience shares my story of living the dream and following my passions, not based on any particular model or structure, but by trying out and experiencing different things and seeing what sticks. Please accept my invitation and join me on my journey:

www.livingbyexperience.com/join

The Freedom Project Online

For me "following the dream" meant traveling the world, and then taking my traveling "self" to who I am at work and at home. I love sharing my experiences with you, and show you how you can live the life you want, increase your passion, reduce stress and fall in love with your life all over again - whether at home, at work, or halfway across the globe. With thousands of students in more countries around the world than I have visited myself, I know there is value in my programs.

If you'd like to learn more, I'd love for you to start with my course "The Freedom Project Online". You'll discover the liberating blueprint to finding freedom and happiness to pursue your biggest dreams, and living life on your terms. This course contains the same information others charge you thousands for... don't miss out! It features my interpretation of the teachings by The Secret, Law of Attraction, Jack Canfield, Dr. Joe Vitale and many others.

Success by nature is a team sport. I'm committed to be a student to those ahead of me, a fellow traveler to those beside me, and a teacher to everybody else. I'm looking forward to see you inside one of my programs. You can join The Freedom Project Online and many other online courses and programs through Liberty Training Academy:

www.libertytrainingacademy.com

The zen approach to travel

I wrote my first book because I wanted to inspire as many people as possible to "just fly", to go travel and see this beautiful planet we live on. The book has inspired many to go travel more and see more of this beautiful planet we live on. And that's what it was all about to begin with.

The importance of my Travel book became clear to me when people attending my art events were drawn to the images that I took on my many travels, and commented on "how they wish they had gone there". A lot of things can get in the way of getting away, but the benefits of travel affect all areas of life.

"Travel is the only thing you can buy that makes you richer"

Unknown

The book has been called the liberating blueprint for finding freedom and happiness in your traveling life. The Freedom Project explains the secrets of travel I continue to use today while exploring the world, and flying for free. You can problably buy a copy of The Freedom Project Travel in the same place as you picked up this book, or directly through the Freedom Project website:

www.freedomprojectbook.com

Letting go and moving on

Too often, I used travel as an escape from a life I didn't even like in the first place. When travelling, I felt less confined by time, money or location. I could do whatever I wanted, I could spend some extra cash I had saved up, and go wherever I wanted to go. Yet after coming home my stress levels quickly spiked back to where they were before I had left. Instead of tacky souvenirs, I wanted to take that experience of freedom home with me. I became passionate about implementing my traveling lifestyle right at home, reconnect with my passions and live a meaningful life.

One of the best things you can do for me is leave a review of my book on Amazon once you bought a copy. It makes a huge difference. It's scary sometimes to throw yourself out there as an author: you pour your heart out on paper for the entire world to see.

Here's a slightly shortened version of a review that one of my readers left. It summarizes quite well what I intended to accomplish with my Happiness book:

> "His story shows us his own courage of starting over and having the drive to act in terms of his own happiness. An inspiring story about struggle and triumph as Wilko takes us on a journey through his own successes and failures. He shows us that the human spirit is powerful through his own experiences. The real challenge of growth comes when you get knocked down. His

story shows us his own courage of starting over and having the drive to act in terms of his own happiness and what it means to him. Everyone has their own story and this book will inspire you to look deep within yourself to find who you truly are, be happy with the journey, face the struggles and have the courage to act on your dreams. Superb read!"

The book shares my journey from dead-end career to living a fulfilling life. If you know anyone that could use a little more happiness in his or her work life, please order them a copy of my book today. And don't forget to get one for yourself, too.

www.freedomprojectbook.com

My ode to Canada

Canada has been called one of the most beautiful countries on earth, and I would have to agree. Photographing the stunning beauty of this country has made me feel more inspired than ever before. I've had close encounters with bears, roamed mountain roads lead by a pack of wolves, and I found many others little tiny wonders of nature. My experiences have all given me a strong bond with these animals and their surroundings I now call home.

I'm a passionate traveller, an artist whose workplace is the road. My photographic art is my way of giving some of my memories back to the world. To experience my photography for yourself, visit:

www.creativewindmill.com

"Photography is not what you see. It is what you allow others to see."

Unknown

My photography book A View to Take Home is a celebration of life in Canada, in all its forms. For many years I braved the rugged and sometimes unpredictable terrain of the Canadian Rocky Mountains to bring home a memorable collection of high-quality photographs. Using my sensitive nature I was able to approach many wildlife creatures in their natural habitat and capture their personality in a beautiful, candid photograph.

A View to Take Home presents the unique life found in the Canadian Rocky Mountains, as well as the bordering cities Calgary and Vancouver. It also includes some of my unseen coastal work from Vancouver Island. Readers will get up-close and personal with grizzly bears, wolves, and much more. A View to Take Home counts over 200 full-color pages containing hundreds of museum quality images. Get yours today:

www.viewtotakehome.com

The photographs I share with you carry one important invitation: to go and see it all for yourself. It is my hope that the stories and images I share with you will inspire you to create your own adventure.

Thank you again, Canada, for everything.

Write A Book

There are a lot of budding authors out there. You might be one of them. But there aren't enough who are truly committed to the dream of making their book a reality.

Writing a Book may not seem simple right away—but it can be. With the perfect balance of information, instruction, and examples, this multimedia learning experience features five modules, well over 70 on-demand videos, and a mixture of worksheets, guides, blog posts, webinars and more. And all of it is designed to deliver you an unparalleled author education experience.

Whether you're an existing author looking to refresh your book marketing skills, learn new trends, and find fresh strategic inspiration, or you're a new author with just a burning desire to "one day" write a book—you're in good hands. Consider joining my author and book writing program today:

www.writeabookinaweek.com

About the author

Wilko van de Kamp is a bestselling author, award-winning photographic artist, and professional world traveler. He has spent his life traveling the world to capture awe-inspiring images for those who wouldn't see them otherwise – and to inspire others to embark on their journey of a lifetime. Through his art, writing and appearances as a keynote speaker he enjoys sharing his colorful experiences with the world.

Wilko was born in the Netherlands, and currently lives in Calgary, Canada. His inspiration comes from traveling all over the world: he calls the Rocky Mountains his "home", and rest of the world his "office". Visit him online at **www.wilko.ca**.

"I fell in love with the exceptional things I saw and the remarkable people who crossed my path."

Wilko van de Kamp